Praise for *Painting Pictures:*
Reframing the World of Inner-City Youth

"Picture this: a gut-wrenching book by an activist who paints a portrait of empowerment and encourages his readers to do the same. Corey D. James presents an unvarnished look at urban life in his inspiring new book "Painting Pictures" which immediately captures readers attention with horrific stories of children being ruthlessly gunned down and the notorious school to prison pipeline that plagues urban communities coast to coast, It's astonishing to think that the author is talking about daily life in an American city but "Painting Pictures" is no sob story. Corey grabs readers by the throat and the heart and gives them tools to DO SOMETHING. Each chapter concludes with creative suggestions to paint a brighter picture... but the true gem of this book is how readers will turn their paintbrushes into meaningful action and guide young people out of the darkness and into the light."
Cheryl Wills, Nationally recognized award-winning television personality and author, "The Emancipation of Grandpa Sandy Wills" & "Die Free: A Heroic Family Tale"

"If you have ever felt hopeful but helpless, driven yet misguided, ready to take on the world except unsure of your purpose; Corey's story can help your picture emerge. Through his personal and moving journey of self-discovery and dedication to youth, one will reflect on our purpose in life. If it is serving young people who are simply looking for champions in their corner, his "take action" recommendations can propel you into the fight over our children's futures."
Aramis Gutierrez, Director of Rutgers Future Scholars

"Corey James' experiences working in our nation's poorest communities demonstrate how neighborhood people with credentials of smart street sense and caring make the most solid contribution to helping young people

who are otherwise forgotten. Mr. James has also made a greater contribution by writing about his meaningful experiences in a direct and powerful way so that we may be prepared and empowered to understand and help many other young people who are so deserved of our attention, but rarely get it."
Jeff Fleischer, CEO of Youth Advocate Programs

"Corey James has a real heart for our youth growing up in at risk environments. This book is both heartbreaking and hopeful. It gives needed insight and a clear challenge to help paint a new picture of beauty and life. I recommend this for mentors and all who are willing to step up and make a difference."
Robert Cruver, Founder & Executive Director of Urban Impact

"James' ability to connect with readers through his emotional and real-life narratives is phenomenal and provides transparency to an audience not keen on the conditions of inner-city neighborhoods. Painting Pictures delivers a gripping message that inspires its readers to consider the challenging norms confronting inner-city communities. Most importantly, this book invokes a call to action that is impossible to ignore."
Jay Barnett, Motivational Speaker and Author, "Finding Our Lost Kings and Queens" and "Letters to a Young Queen"

"Each of us, at some time in life, needs a helping hand. We are reminded of this in Painting Pictures. It is a powerful and deeply spiritual book. It is about loss and hope and abandonment and connection. James is passionate about mentoring and illustrates its compassionate and redemptive power. He refuses to accept as normal what typically results in poverty stricken neighborhoods and through mentorship fights to shape hopeful futures for young people so that they rise above an "insidious culture of violence that cheapens human life". In each chapter, he challenges us to reflect and plan how we can help a young person. He challenges us to care, to see that the life of young people born to poverty and violence indeed can be different than what is typical. With

our helping hand young people can do much better than "to live beneath their potential". Reading this book will charge you to make a difference."
Dr. Arthur B. Powell, Department Chair & Associate Professor of Urban Education, Rutgers University

Corey James writes, "the best masterpieces are those that are reworked and created from what has been rejected or considered unusable." Painting Pictures is both a resource and inspiration for mentors, community leaders, friends, relatives and individuals looking for hope in messy and miserable life situations. It offers stories of redemption and principles for restoration. I highly recommend Painting Pictures.
Dr. David Stefan, Director of Behavioral & Social Sciences, Indiana Wesleyan University

"Painting Pictures is a clarion call to all adults as a reminder to not give up on our young people ever. It is a reminder to all of us that just as God does not use our past to determine our future neither should we. We are all being commissioned by this book to step up and step into the lives of those who are being marginalized by society. We must never forget that for so many of us who have achieved some modicum of success that our lives would have turned out much differently. It is our duty to respond to this call!!!"
Reverend Cynthia D. Jackson, Pastor of Allen AME Church, Newark, NJ and Judge of Jersey City Municipal Court

"This book informs a framework for the better making of black men and boys. I'm reminded of so much of myself in these young men and why I have a particular passion for seeing the best in the mentees I have established relationships with over the years. I especially appreciate the call to "paint a picture" after each story - because to whom much is given, much is required. This is an enriching compilation of meaningful real-life context followed by a challenge for all of us to continue to lift as we climb."
Okey K. Enyia, CBCF Urban Health Public Policy Fellow

Painting Pictures

Reframing the World of Inner-City Youth

COREY D. JAMES

DEDICATION

In memory of three amazing women who painted pictures for me: my grandmother, great aunt, and godmother.

Mabel Lee Wilson
Ollie Faye Adams
Mary Ann Fowler

They are gone but impossible to forget as they show up in many of my thoughts, my words and my actions. I am who I am because of them. While I wish they were here to see this project, I know that before they left this earth, they were already proud of me. This gives me great joy.

This book is also dedicated to every young person who feels like life has been unfair to them; who feels like they are living in a dead end. I not only dedicate this book to those young people, I also dedicate my life to the purpose of showing them greater possibilities and painting pictures for them as they were painted for me.

CONTENTS

INTRODUCTION: A DIFFERENT WORLD

"Did you hear about the rose that grew
from a crack in the concrete?
Proving nature's laws wrong it
learned to walk without having feet."

- Tupac Shakur

It is a common saying that a person is a product of their environment. And a person's environment establishes values, rules, and culture. So then, what happens when a child's environment is dominated by crime, violence, and poverty? These are the circumstances in which many of our youth struggle to survive, and it is a population that illustrates a vast socio-cultural gap. So often we live in our own little world in a bubble, completely unaware of the lifestyle of those in disadvantaged neighborhoods. But it is important to understand the world our youth grow up in. Imagine innocent children growing up in neighborhoods akin to warzones. Imagine cracked streets lined with broken or abandoned buildings housing drug addicted vagrants and their pitiless dope dealers. Imagine homes plagued with all sorts of vermin and not enough food to feed a family. Of course in some cases this is hyperbole, but compared to what is needed in order to grow a child into a successful adult, we must advocate for our urban youth and teach them to paint better pictures for themselves.

While the impact of an advocate can be immeasurable, it is still important to know that inner-city youth grow up in an entirely different world than those in middle class society, and their experience in the world has far more daunting obstacles to overcome. That is also what makes these youth special. While there are stories of tragedy, there are also stories of triumph and redemption. Here is one such story written by the youth himself:

"I grew up in the slums of Newark, New Jersey and in the depths of poverty. My background paralleled that of an at-risk youth statistic. I was an African-American boy, raised in a single parent household. Though the word, "household," doesn't capture the image of my upbringing. Half my family was drug users, including my dope fiend father, who persistently abused my mother both physically and emotionally. My mother, my older brother and myself, were homeless for countless years. Sometimes we'd wander the streets in the middle of the night waiting on a friend or family member to call my mother's cell and allow us to sleep at their home. We've lived in every shelter in and around Newark, from the YMCA to the homeless shelter in Irvington. We migrated from my mother's friends' apartment, to distant family members' apartments. I can't count how many times we slept bunched up on hardwood floors, sleeping at five o'clock in the morning just to wake up at seven o'clock for school. The truth is that most of those midnight expeditions were attempts to escape danger. My mother was a victim of domestic violence in damn near every relationship she entered. Seldom did I see my mom without at least a bruise on her face. I often asked questions about our lifestyle, as kids do, but my mother never explained anything. And

although I loved my mother, I knew love was my limit. I knew I couldn't protect my mother, thus being away from her and being distracted in anyway served as a remedy for my limitations. I began to hate 'home', even when we had our own house after years of waiting on our Government Housing assignment to go through. She was never able to understand or even care how much my brother and I hated the lifestyle. My resentment of being at 'home' or even being around my mother grew rapidly. However, as a child, I found my salvation in school. I was the biggest troublemaker and class clown. Although I didn't do well in any subjects, except art and math, I still enjoyed school and the acknowledgement by my peers, teachers, principals and even janitors. Schoolwork didn't always excite me, but I loved being in a place where everyone knew me and gave me attention.

It wasn't enough though. I dreaded going home after school, where I would find my crackhead uncle, who always stole my clothes, my mother's change, and even our TV. I dreaded my mother telling me another one of my cousins, uncles, or aunts got murdered. Isolation and freedom from home was like heroin to me. My mother never had strict control over my brother and me; she worked at Pathmark during the day and drank herself to sleep at night. The Southward section of Newark was populated with all my cousins, halfbrothers, and stepbrothers. This gave my brother and me a chance to play around in the neighborhood, hang out on the project roofs and ball up at the court till late night. I heard the sound of gunshots and stolen cars literally every night, but that was the norm. My brother and I used to peak out the window to try and see what car it was or to see the person who got shot. My brother was a year older and during middle school, he was only interested in getting girls. I was too, but I was more into getting money, fresh white V-necks, and chilling with my homies from the block. My homies and I were like brothers to each other. It makes

3

sense why we bonded. I remember at least ten of those friends, who in just the 7th grade, had at least one dead brother or one dead father who was killed around the neighborhood. This violence didn't stop me from going outside though. I was too intrigued by the fast money I saw being made by the old heads, grown-ups, and even my peers. I always wore hand-me-downs from my brother and barely owned anything new except a yearly pair of school sneakers. My half-brother, who was a year older than me, noticed that I wanted money. He knew how life was treating me, for he was a victim too. By sixth grade I start hanging out with him, smoking weed and Blacks. The next year however, changed my life and shaped my destiny. I was slowly becoming desensitized to their lifestyle.

In 7th grade, I began selling my half-brother's weed to eighth graders during school and everyone in and out of school respected me more. The lifestyle was one I cherished. In school, it helped in every way. More girls liked me, all while still maintaining decent grades. What complicated this lifestyle was an opportunity and the first of its kind in my life. Upon the completion of a five year commitment, there was a program that guaranteed a scholarship to a four year University without spending a dime. Only a small percentage of 7th graders are admitted based on a range of criteria. As a seventh grader, I could only remember being forced to do the application. And the following summer, I was accepted into this new one of a kind program. My mother wasn't knowledgeable about college stuff, so she would wake me up Saturday mornings for the program. The program opened my eyes up to things I had never seen before. I remember just wishing my brother and half-brothers were able to witness it with me, but being around peers that didn't respect me pushed me to ditch the program. There were many students in this program and I was confident I wouldn't have been missed. My mother basically went with my decision. Sometimes I'd lie about what I was doing and most of the times she'd believe me. I truly enjoyed the life of a drug dealer. I had new gear every day in eighth grade. I had new shirts, new jeans, and even got my ear pierced. My mother knew I was selling weed because of my new stuff. She started checking me while I was asleep and dozens of times found weed and a little bit of cash in my jeans. She'd put me on punishment but that was about it. I felt good about myself and never regretted my decision to ditch that program.

One day in May of my eighth grade year, I was called into the guidance counselor's office. I saw my mother, my guidance counselor, and this young woman staring dead into my eyes without a smile. Her name was Ms. Anderson. I got in trouble very often, being a victim of countless suspensions. Yet none of my disciplinary staff have ever looked at me the way Ms. Anderson did. Her glare was defined by disappointment and optimism. Ms. Anderson explained vital points to my mother about the program, explaining its unmatched benefits and support. She briefed my mother on college in general; to make sure she stayed on me about attending the program. I was a bit angry, but I didn't care that much, barely listening to their conversation. At the end of the meeting, Ms. Anderson told me, "I can tell you're a leader. And by the way, once you're a part of 'the program' you'll always be a part of 'the program.'" That moment alone, carves my daily actions today. What Ms. Anderson did for me gave me a reason to impress her. Her simple acknowledgement felt real, as if she really saw potential in me for the future. As a kid it was hard to fathom, but I knew I wanted to impress her from then on. I think most people can sense disingenuous comments. We all know most parents, teachers, and even counselors say inspiring things out of pity, or even give you goals that were challenging, made for the "get-by." However, Ms. Anderson and the team of mentors who ran the program challenged me during the duration of the five-year program. They made me conscious of my dreams and desires. Dreams that weren't too far to grasp, yet distant enough that you'll have to stretch far beyond your comfort zone to reach them.

However, this paradise wasn't every day, and an everyday escape was necessary for me during my time at Westside High School and living in the Westward. I knew no one in the surrounding neighborhoods. My brother and I were robbed and robbed others. We knew we had to fight our way up and take whatever was given. I expected to go to Weequahic (High School) in the southward, but I ended up at Westside. I didn't know a soul. My brother knew some people, but I was still forced to gain my own popularity, notoriety, and my own stain. Because I was unknown, I was tested more times than I can count. I was involved in dozens of fights and had been jumped a couple of times. Additionally, during this time, my mother had surgery and was barely home, so I had to take care of my brothers all the time, often skipping school to do so. My older brother and I were always in conflict with my mother's friends who lived with us. We fought them so much we had to move to north Newark with my aunt. Eventually, I found myself without any family support, except my Program and sports. But neither was sufficient. I needed friends that would have my back, especially in a school split into so many different pieces. Everyone was banging from Bloods and Crips, to rival street gangs. One day I was walking home from wrestling practice when two dudes tried to strong-arm me. I was fighting them off for a long time until eventually my classmate, a well-known banger, laughed as he told them that I was good and that I was the homie. He came up to me and said "come on cuh, I'll spark you up." From there, I was officially introduced to selling dope and crack, holding pistols and the gang life; I was introduced to my family. However, I noticed that the more people I befriended under my set, more of my friends were murdered. Every day a homie was shot, and every other day a homie was killed. Even the people making fast money and only selling drugs were dying. I then understood that I didn't want to die.

We eventually moved to a housing project in north Newark. I hated that side of Newark. Even my brothers, who had turned Blood, were getting robbed and jumped a lot. I started to stay over-night in the hallways of our trap house after school because the walk and bus ride home was too dangerous, due to the set I was banging. I'd seen people bleed out from gun wounds in that hallway; I've seen death. Yet in order to keep my composure, I thought about my program. I knew I didn't want to die and after my mentors started coming to my school to talk with me, to pick me up, and be the family I tried so desperately to create with my set, I realized that college was my only salvation. The fact that I was at my program spending time with my mentors 2 -3 days a week, and I still was inseparable from the street life, shows the pull it has on inner-city youth. I skipped school a lot, did all kinds of drugs and struggled during my years in High school. I was very smart though, scoring extremely high on exams, though it didn't translate to my grades. My hood started to break down due to a major crackdown on drugs, leaving my main block in shambles. And my homies were still dying. I knew school was the only choice; however, I had mediocre grades that didn't reflect my potential. This made my dream and my destiny that Ms. Anderson told me about out of reach. I wasn't going to get my scholarship. After applying to the university I was rejected, I had the university tattooed all over me but it meant nothing anymore. I felt like nothing, a blank.

However, my mentors never left my side and every other person in my program fought for me persistently. The fight paid off, giving me a chance at a college education and more importantly, a degree free of charge. Where am I now? I'm at a renowned State University. I'm a thriving junior reaching feats I never thought I'd attain. Some would ask me, "Is it challenging?" "Is it time consuming?" "Do you sometimes wish you weren't here?" Most likely, I would answer yes to them all. And if you ask the majority of inner-city youth this same question, they might not even have an answer because they weren't given the opportunity to try. With the opportunity I've been provided, I've widened my knowledge and learned to combine humility, optimism and perseverance. I'm not the same person I was years ago. I have changed and though I do resent the things I've participated in, I don't regret them. My experiences, in combination with the education I'm currently receiving, are the ingredients for creating a leader. I lost my half-brother, who was in the same grade as I, to gun violence during my time in college. Opportunities are limited but I always think to myself, "what if he was the one that got into the program?" Or what if some of my friends and family who are gone had received similar opportunities? They were just like me: minority, poor, and from dysfunctional homes. They also came from hoods plagued by death, drugs, and money. They were tattooed since a young age, shot pistols and sold dope for a living. They gang banged and smoked weed to fight the demons and perhaps still held great potential within them. The only difference is that I'm alive and a successful college student. Most importantly, the difference is that I had the opportunity to be and do those things. We are truly all one family, friend, or mentor away from success.

If I was given up on and not given opportunities, who knows where I would be today? Probably still selling dope on my avenue or maybe in the state prison. Or I'd be at my mother's house living off her food stamps and a dead end job, or shot dead like my brother. I'm not in those places, and I can't give up on our youth because someone cared enough to not give up on me. Someone cared enough to rescue me from depths that appeared inescapable. Someone gave me a chance to succeed. Now let's give this generation a chance. They are filled with creativity and passion for life. If we give up on that one child, we give up on our future."

Signed,
the Rose that grew from concrete

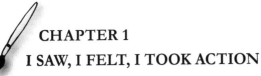

CHAPTER 1
I SAW, I FELT, I TOOK ACTION

"No person was ever honored for what he received. Honor has been the reward for what he gave."

- Calvin Coolidge

I showed up to my first client's house while he and his father were in a fiery argument. The young man - who wasn't in the habit of engaging in arguments for very long - pulled a gun from his waistband. At this moment I believed my first day on the job would be my last day on earth. I would be lying if I said I wasn't scared. (Scared was an understatement). My life flashed before me and every cell in my body burned with an anxious terror. It was my job to advocate for this young man. So, too involved to run and too nervous to do anything else, I did nothing but witness the violent frustration of a young black adolescent. I wasn't trained for this moment, but I finally gathered my thoughts and said something that was perhaps meaningful. Somehow I found the ability to diffuse the situation and provide intervention. I took the young man with me and we descended several floors down a dark and narrow stairwell riddled with misplaced mats, splintered wood and rusted nails sticking out from the side. We sat outside and talked under a starry

Atlantic City night. We talked about what made him so angry at his father, about what events led him to where he currently is, and about where he would like to be years into the future. We then went back inside and spoke with his father, which resulted in mediation. Where did I learn this? I didn't. I don't remember my thoughts after this situation. They were blurred by the threat of this experience. What I do remember is that I had busted into a world of frustration and constant aggression, a more hostile environment than I was used to. I didn't quit though; I stayed with it. I continued to meet with this young man several times a week, month after month. He and I worked together to reenroll him in school, obtain a job, and make better daily decisions. This young man became one of my greatest success stories, and is the reason I began a journey that I never imagined - or desired.

Never did I think I would be an advocate for urban youth. Who would've thought that I'd develop a fondness for young people that society had named 'criminals,' 'gangsters,' 'thugs,' 'drug pushers,' 'jail birds.' But boy did it find me, grab hold of me, and not let go. I wake, eat, and sleep thinking about how I might better impact the lives of marginalized youth. Where did this passion and desire come from? I do not know. Oftentimes people are most passionate about what they themselves have experienced. A rape victim is more likely to become an advocate for that population. A cancer survivor is likely to create programming for cancer patients. A person who has come from the streets, made mistakes, and overcame those mistakes is more likely to go back and encourage other young people going down the same path to make better choices, re-create their lives, and paint better pictures. This was not so for me; thus I've had some apprehension and feelings of inadequacy regarding the passion that keeps me awake at night. I thought: how can I be effective if I never experienced street life, incarceration, or the poverty that would cause one to feel forced to take illegal methods to survive, or even the high that drugs give to numb the hardships of life? I found myself stuck between my experiences and my passion. Oh sure I've experienced pain, tragedy, turmoil, poverty, hopeless moments, (life hasn't been any bed of roses for me). However, it hasn't been the same experience as many inner-city youth and not for the same reasons. What I have learned is that in order to impact the life of a young person, it's not about similar experiences, body counts, or how much time you served in prison. It's about how much you care. One may believe that this population doesn't want the love and support of advocate programs or passionate mentors because of their tough demeanors and experiences. Yet I guarantee that if, as a mentor, you show that you authentically care -which they can tell- then you will make a huge impact regardless of your background. I care deeply about my clients - underprivileged youths - and that compassion has been the fundamental component to success in my field.

While it is true that one's heart is the greatest component needed to reach these youth, I continued to ask myself why? What am I doing here? Why am I doing this? How did my heart become so attached to this mission? Others who knew me and my background would ask the same question of me, but all I could provide in response was that it felt good to help. As I considered these questions, I learned that the more involved I became with inner-city youth, the more these questions were being answered in my own head. And even the answers themselves became more defined as I experienced the stories of these young men and women. When at first I thought I was an outsider intruding into lives that I knew little about, I realized I had more in common with them that I help than I originally thought. When at first I thought I was unfit to identify with them and that it took an unwitting audacity for someone like me, who didn't grow up in the hood surrounded by drugs and violence, to even try to relate to them, I realized that just maybe there was some of me in them and perhaps more of them in me than I ever knew. This point was made clear to me when I had a conversation with a young man after one of our group sessions. I hadn't expected to uncover any new information about myself, but listening to him vent his frustrations and hearing him articulate his dreams reminded me of the emotions I felt when I was younger. In fact, I would assert that we can all relate to a certain amount of youthful frustration and longing. The young man didn't look like the typical troubled youth who wore their toughness for all to see. He was quiet and reserved but articulate and seemed to be much more reflective than his fellow participants in the program. Whereas others did not question their environment or lifestyle as abnormal, he was aware that the cycle of cruelty he grew up in was wrong and that he deserved more. For this young man, his frustrations stemmed from growing up in a household with constant conflict. His family, though they lived together, was fragmented and each piece was constantly at odds with the other. The young man began selling drugs and rarely came home at night, and although I never turned to any criminal activities, I saw a very real part of myself in this young man. I too felt like I deserved better. Yes, that's what it was; it was my heart that was drawn to these young people because I too was a kid who felt unloved, stuck, and broken. Not because I didn't have support, but because I didn't have the support of a "traditional family." Whether or not all the parts are there - a mother, father, brother and sister - a traditional family is supposed to be bonded together by unconditional love, kindness, and support. I always felt like something was missing from my life, a vital component to my well-being, but I could never articulate what it was. However, working with many of these young people and seeing the results of a dysfunctional family, I too realized that my own wounds were still plaguing me from being brought up in a fragmented home. Much like the young man I spoke to, even as a child, I felt I knew I deserved more. The few memories I have of my mother and father together were moments of verbal and physical abuse. I remember clothes being flung out the window, furniture being thrown in rage, keys being hidden so we couldn't go anywhere. Such egregious manipulation and aggressive behavior in one's own family has a long-lasting effect, and I hate to see it within any family. The mayhem and destruction within a place that was supposed to be home was something I could not tolerate growing up in, so I didn't. I spent much of my childhood growing up with my grandmother. There I lived a caring and sheltered life that I am always grateful for but even with my grandma, I always wondered what it would be like to have a normal family. I knew I wanted what I saw my peers at school had: parents who came to support at sports games, concerts, and parent/teacher conferences. I ached for the typical family vacations where we would bond and make memories together. I didn't have that, so I felt in many ways abandoned and rejected. The more I worked with these youth, the more they shared their stories, the more I learned about myself. I too was the kid who didn't expect to live past 20. Not because I thought I would be killed on the streets, but because I wanted to end my own life. I too had a bad outlook on my future like many of our youth do, another similarity I found. Then most profoundly, I realized that like the young people I work with, I hid it. I hid it not with a tough demeanor, but for me with a quiet demeanor. I became very timid. I took on the good kid behavior and stayed to myself. Some saw this as me being a well behaved child, but the truth was that I was disguising myself because underneath I was broken, wounded and struggling to find a place in this world. I chose not to find my place with gangs and the street life, but I still had the feeling of being misplaced, similar to youth surrounded by negative influences. I learned that my passion really wasn't something that came out of the blue, but that it rose from my childhood and manifested itself in the knowledge and satisfaction I received from devoting myself to assisting those in damaged communities. However, my career in the field did not start with such devotion and passion.

When I was offered a job to work with the juvenile justice population, my immediate reaction was nope, not at all, I can't do that. However, I also disliked the job I held at that time, so it didn't take a lot to sway me to take the position. Plus it was a financial raise that I desperately needed. It was something to do until something better came along, I thought. It being a field job with a break from the office, with flexibility and better pay sounded good to me. However, I was extremely nervous. I was a sheltered kid that never even went to New York City and lived 30 minutes away from it until I was grown. The kid that had to be home by the time the street lights were on and couldn't do anything or go anywhere that might expose me to the dangers of the world. The guy who had no demeanor of toughness, being raised in a family of loving motherly figures, is now considering a job working in the community where young black and Latino kids are raised by the streets. Young people with legitimate anger issues who are active members of dangerous gangs and consistently involve themselves in gang activity: stealing cars, selling drugs, raiding homes, brandishing guns. They would be my clients and those who I'd have the responsibility to advocate for. So if I were to say the wrong thing, it would be over for me, I thought. I was out of my lane. Was I really though?

This job required me to go into the homes of clients on house arrest with ankle monitors shackled to their feet and provide intervention. I was going into homes that were quite literally broken, dilapidated and infested with roaches (I had to learn how to do the shaking dance after leaving homes), but that was the easy part.

These were the neighborhoods police themselves would not go to without appropriate support. Of course, I could never tell my family that this was my occupation because even after becoming an adult, I was still being treated like a kid. My grandmother and great aunt who were still living when I began this journey would've had a fit. I was having an internal fit myself. Still, with much fear, courage, but mostly fear, I began a job I thought I'd do for only a little while.

So you've already heard how that first day went. It went bad. Really bad. I brought my materials prepared to have an organized and meaningful session of goal setting, but that wasn't the way it went. After this first experience, I considered asking for my old job back – the one I hated so much with less money and no flexibility. It was just that bad. I kept at it though. As difficult and emotionally taxing as it was, I never believed in quitting, or perhaps my heart was beginning to find its purpose that day. While I still wasn't sure what I was doing or how I could be most effective, my heart was learning and loving and saw opportunities for true impact.

Before then, I never imagined the profound impact I could have on a young person raised by the streets. I began this journey so detached from that world in my overly sheltered life; I didn't know or understand the pain, the constant struggle, or the war being faced daily. I learned that day.

I've come to understand that I have been blessed with a burden, a burden of passion and optimism. I devoted myself intensively to providing results, so it became an obsession for me to see youth succeed in these neighborhoods. Many times I wanted it more than them. I began to see the commitment pouring into my personal life. I received phone calls in the middle of the night from youths and parents. The youths wanted more time with me after my service hours were completed and I would agree, realizing that this would keep them out of trouble. They became like extended relatives, inviting me to family events and gatherings. I became a highly requested advocate, like a big brother, uncle, friend, and father to many. It became a life I thoroughly enjoyed that provided a meaningful sense of satisfaction.

I've seen young people make 180 degree turns. I've heard parents acknowledge that their child is a changed person. I've seen the little boy or little girl disguised under the tough demeanor become a kid again. With the good, however, you also experience the bad. I've experienced the tragedies of the streets. I've known youth that were not able to break despairing generational cycles. I've received phone calls stating that my client (who is now my family) was incarcerated again, shot, stabbed or even worse, murdered. I've been to more funerals for young people than I would like to count. I've cried over lives of young people that I knew well, and I've cried over lives that I never met. I cannot simply cry over it and talk about it only. It frustrates me greatly to hear people talk about what's happening in these communities, wear t-shirts of what's happening, post on social media the realities of the streets, yet do nothing about it.

A few years ago, I was invited to a Martin Luther King Jr. celebration, honoring the legacy of justice and social activism that the great freedom fighter represents. The keynote speaker delivered a poignant speech, discussing a passage in scripture in the book of Nehemiah. His points were that Nehemiah saw, he felt, and took action. What happened to me that day, I do not know. I cried like a child as the speaker conveyed his message. I felt like Nehemiah. I saw how our communities had been ruined by drug infestation, homicide, and gangs. I've seen how young black kids have had to take on the behaviors of their environment just to survive and become something they are not. I've seen the pain in their faces, the hurt, and their silent cry.

I felt it heavy in my heart, the truth of the sermon and the burden it bared. It felt heavy not because it truly impacted my day to day. Not because it impacted those that I was most close to, but I felt strongly, as if it was me, as if Nehemiah's call to action was my own. It felt as if the blood spilled in the streets was my blood and I had never felt anything like that before. I've had moments of passion in other areas, but they all weakened over time. This had been the only cause that I felt so strongly about that it made me weep for a kid I barely knew.

> It felt as if the blood spilled in the streets was my blood and I had never felt anything like that before.

Author, John C. Maxwell says, "When you identify what makes you cry, and you tap into it, you receive a major piece of the puzzle for your purpose your why, and begin seeing your pathway to a life that matters."

I saw and I felt, but I knew that seeing and feeling without action is tragedy.

So I took action. When I heard this message on Martin Luther King Jr. Day, I was already working in the community and serving youth, and doing all I could. Or so I believed, but my heart said, *you can do more. There are more lives to impact, more destinies to change.* I cried because I was heartbroken over the tragedies I'd seen, but I also cried because I was joyful over the successes I'd experienced. One of my mentees was with me that day and looked at me with tears in his eyes too and said "That's what you've done for me, you came and got me." To this day, this young man will refer to me as Mr. Miyagi, as he considers me his coach and his hero.

> I saw and I felt, but I knew that seeing and feeling without action is tragedy.

So here I am taking action, married to the cause till death us do part. Though not because they're dying... they're supposed to bury me – not I bury them.

Will you, along with me, help this generation paint better pictures?

Painting Pictures Challenge: As you read this book, I challenge you to consider the dreadful conditions that plague our young people, and how these conditions make you feel. Does it make you want to take action or do nothing? If you answered take action, consider ways you can help. If you answered do nothing, I'm sure it's not because you're a bad person. You may feel inadequate or think you don't have enough time or resources. I want to encourage you to know that you are all a young person needs. You don't need money, or a lot of materials. You just need a little bit of the time you think you don't have. I promise, you do have time to impact a young person. Ultimately, we decide what we do with our time. The Juvenile Offenders and Victims 2014 National report states: "Law enforcement agencies in the U.S. made 1.6 million arrests of persons under age 18 in 2010." The time you can provide to a young person really does matter.

delinquency on their own. For those who have more trouble, Elliott has shown that establishing a relationship with a significant other (a partner or mentor) as well as employment correlates with youthful offenders of all races "aging out" of delinquent behavior as they reach young adulthood.

Impacting the life of a troubled youth is like the game of Spades, one hand doesn't determine the win. It's a culmination of hands that results in the big win. Some hands 'we' will win, and other hands 'we' will lose, but regardless of if we win or lose, 'we' encourage our partner to continue on and we continue on too.

It is hard to see a young person appear to make progress then regress. Still, it happens and it happens often. The greatest tragedy is for a person to enter the life of an at-risk youth and then walk out because it doesn't seem to be working, or it's not happening fast enough. This forms another layer of resistance for them because it is a pattern that has happened to them too many times. People walk in and people walk out.

As I'm writing, I get a call from the parent of a young man I've been working with for several years. He's been making great strides, and he's turned over a new leaf. I was just sharing his success stories last week with family and friends saying that I almost don't recognize him. Then today, I get a call that says he's been arrested. Months of winning, even with poor hands being dealt, and this hand 'we' lose. While it's disappointing and it hurts, it doesn't mean I have any lost love or that I'm done mentoring him. Nope, it means that I have more mentoring to do. I refuse to be that partner I talked about who gets up in the middle of the game and quits on their partner for making a mistake or for the lost. It makes your partner never want to play again. We can't do that in this game. If we, as their 'partners,' resign because of the losses, we simply push them further and further down the road of despair and destruction. We must stay and finish the game no matter how long it takes because 'we' win or lose together. We're on the same team.

President Barack Obama said it simply: "All a young person needs is knowing that somebody cares about them and believes in them."

Painting Pictures Challenge: Team up with a young person who's having trouble playing the game. Teach them the rules and strategies of how to win regardless of the obstacles, setbacks, and pain. Be the type of partner that refuses to see them fail. Go the extra mile and help in ways that friends and family may not understand. Go out on a limb for them. This is my challenge to you.

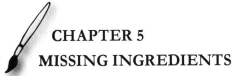

CHAPTER 5
MISSING INGREDIENTS

"Kids have a hole in their soul in the shape of their dad. And if a father is unwilling or unable to fill that hole, it can leave a wound that is not easily healed."

- Roland Warren

I attended the funeral of an eighty-seven year old man who was celebrated for being an incredible father. His sons and daughter reflected on stories of their father's incredible support, his love and his discipline. They had precious memories of him being a provider, protector, and coach for the family. A friend of the family made remarks at the service and said, "This man raised three sons and one daughter and none of them have been arrested. All of them have become remarkable adults, god-fearing and admirable." His own son gave the eulogy and he stated, "I am who I am because of my daddy. He didn't leave us with a lot of money, he didn't leave us with any land, he didn't leave us with a lot of material stuff but he left us with some tools. Not the many screw drivers he owned, or his wrenches, not the drills and carpentry tools that he had since the 1940's... but the greatest tool he left was his voice. This voice will continue to speak."

This service reminded me of the vital role of a father. For the next several days, I began to reflect on the power of a father's voice. Society often under-acknowledges the father's importance. Mother's day is more celebrated than father's day. Mothers are more highly regarded but does the father matter?

First, I considered human physiology. To say it simply, in order for pregnancy to occur the egg has to meet a healthy sperm. Therefore, while the egg (the mother) is important, the sperm (the father) is equally important. One cannot produce without the other. And while many sperm, between 40 million and 600 million, are released during intercourse, only one sperm is needed to fertilize the egg.

WebMD takes a look at the facts about Sperm, "Why are so many sperm released if it takes only one to make a baby? To meet the waiting egg, the semen must travel from the vagina to the fallopian tubes, an arduous journey that few sperm survive. For those that complete the trip, penetration of the egg is far from a sure thing. The egg is covered by a thick layer that makes fertilization difficult. Experts believe this process may be nature's way of allowing only the healthiest sperm to fertilize the egg, thereby providing the best chances to produce a healthy baby."

I would like to consider that thought, "When the healthiest sperm fertilizes the egg chances are greater to produce a healthy baby." The egg doesn't just need any old sperm, but a healthy sperm is needed. A healthy sperm is one that moves and is active. And if one active and moving sperm reaches the egg, it makes a world of difference in the ability to produce.

So, why do we think it's possible to have a healthy, whole child without the male role, if in human physiology the male is necessary? We hear mothers say, "I'm the mother and the father," suggesting they can raise their child alone. And sure there are plenty of amazing mothers that can, but how does it impact the child when the voice of the father is not there?

> So, why do we think it's possible to have a healthy, whole child without the male role, if in human physiology the male is a must.

Unfortunately, we see what too often happens when the child doesn't have the male voice.

According to the U.S. Census Bureau data 2011:

- *63% of youth suicides are from fatherless homes – 5 times the average*
- *90% of all homeless and runaway children are from fatherless homes – 32 times the average*
- *85% of all children who show behavior disorders come from fatherless homes – 20 times the average*
- *80% of rapists with anger problems come from fatherless homes – 14 times the average*
- *71% of all High school dropouts come from fatherless homes – 9 times the average*
- *75% of all adolescent patients in chemical abuse centers come from fatherless homes – 10 times the average*

- *85% of all youths in prison come from fatherless homes – 20 times the average*

The absence of the male voice in the family household has greatly impacted our society. Just as the process of creating a child requires both male and female, raising a child also requires both a male voice and a female voice. It is important that the males be a part of the entire process, not just the conception of a child.

So what happens when the father isn't there? A key ingredient becomes missing and just as a cake that has insufficient oil will fall, so will many young people without a father. A father is like oil to a cake, the ingredient that acts as a binder, which holds other ingredients together.

> A father is like oil to a cake, the ingredient that acts as a binder, which holds other ingredients together.

As I was at the beautiful ceremony to celebrate the life of an outstanding man who passed at eighty-seven, I thought to myself that so many of our young people are lacking this ingredient. That's why our young people are falling victim to the streets and gangs, dropping out of high school, becoming incarcerated, and buried in cemeteries. A key ingredient is missing.

They see what they shouldn't see, but aren't seeing what they should. We mentioned in previous chapters and will look more deeply into the tragedies their eyes witness. These tragedies occur in the turmoil within their neighborhoods, in their homes, and even in their schools. I believe that if our young people had fathers, it would lessen the impact of the difficult things they do see. Perhaps their environments won't change anytime soon, but with the right voice their lives can change. We need fathers that can take away the 'sting' of the streets for our children. There's a story called "The Bee Sting" that illustrates the power of a father,

A vacationing family drove along in their car, windows rolled down, enjoying the warm summer breeze of the sunny day. All of a sudden a big bumble bee darted in through the window and started buzzing around inside the car. Their little girl, highly allergic to bee stings, cringed in the back seat. If she got stung, she could die within an hour.

"Oh, Daddy," she squealed in terror. "It's a bee! It's going to sting me!"

The father pulled the car over to a stop, and reached back to try to catch the bee. Buzzing around towards him, the bee bumped against the front windshield where the father trapped it in his fist. Holding it in his closed hand, the father waited for the inevitable sting. The bee stung the father's hand and in pain, the father opened his hand and showed his daughter that she had nothing left to fear. He willingly took the sting so that his daughter would not suffer and die.

-Author Unknown

We need fathers that refuse to allow this generation to die, who refuse to bury a generation full of purpose and potential. Denzel Washington, in the movie John Q. said, "I will not bury my son, he will bury me!" We need fathers who understand that their voice is so powerful that it can overcome the negative and not allow the streets to grip many of our youth, as it has.

In the movie, "Boyz in the Hood" of the three young men we follow during this story, Doughboy, Ricki and Tre, Tre was the only one who had the influence of a caring father and for that reason his life looked different than his peers. Early in the movie we find Tre getting into trouble often in school. Tre at this time was living with his mom, and a promise, or threat, was made that if she received one more phone call, he was going to go and move in with his dad. Tre's dad had been requesting to keep his son indefinitely. He said, "It's the job of the father to teach a son how to be a man." So, Tre moves with his father, though still in a bad neighborhood of crime, drugs, and gangs. The only difference now was that he had a father to guide him.

In the movie, we see Tre fishing and lifting weights with his dad. Tre's father was present during moments that Tre was successful, times that he failed and times when he needed to be consoled, especially when his friend was killed. He provided guidance and said things like, "Any fool with a dick can make a baby, but only a real man can raise his children." Tre was provided a role model who exemplified what a "healthy" father looks like, one who supports, cares, and is present emotionally and physically. While Tre still made some bad choices, his destiny was positively impacted because of a loving father. Tre was saved by the voice of his father; he made the better choice when his friends decided to take revenge for their friend's death. Tre, after deciding to participate in the revenge, opted to get out the car and return home. All of his peers ended up dead and Tre went to Morehouse College. A father changed his world.

Our youth need dads to change their world. Unfortunately, many are unknowingly negatively impacted by the lack of a father. They don't realize the impact because it's hard to recognize a missing ingredient if they've never had anything to compare it with. When you're surrounded by an environment of 'fallen cakes,' being lopsided becomes normal. Something is missing, but many don't know what. We were conceived because of a father, so it's natural for our hearts to ache for him. Roland Warren (quoted in the outset of this chapter) said, "Kids have a hole in their soul in the shape of their dad." I was speaking with a 58 year-old woman who was raised by an amazing mother and step father, yet even now her heart aches to know who her biological father is. A missing father is a cry of the heart that cannot be silenced.

I posted a blog on the topic of the negative impact of fatherlessness, and it received the greatest number of responses compared to many other postings. It was as if everyone became a little boy and little girl as they read, conveying how deeply they are hurt because of growing up without a father. The blog was based on a study conducted by Dr. Gabriella Gobbi with mice and found that those mice raised without a father displayed signs of 'abnormal social interactions' and were far more aggressive than mice raised with both parents. The difference was more pronounced in daughters than in sons, and females raised without fathers also had a greater sensitivity to the stimulant drug amphetamine.

The study reported that the behavior of the mice was consistent with studies in children raised without a father, highlighting an increased risk for deviant behavior, criminal activity, substance abuse, impoverished educational performance, and mental illness.

Dr. Gobbi's conclusion was: "Growing up without a father can permanently alter the brain: Fatherless children are more likely to grow up angry and turn to drugs."

The blogging world agreed with many heartfelt responses:

"I am a 28 year old female who still struggles with the absence of my father. I'm trying not to cry as I write this but is there any hope for me? How do I reconstruct my brain to be better, not angry and to trust? Please help if you can."

"Until the age of 24, I never knew how to be 'just friends' with a guy. I never had a father-figure so no one taught me how to innocently love a man. I was that girl who people talked about. You know, the girl who called guys her brothers but would turn around and possibly sleep with them. I didn't know better. I thought every guy was fair game and that there is no such thing as a girl having a male friend. I had to get hurt numerous times to learn. It's true that pain is the best teacher. Not having a father-figure or father at all, taught me how to be the ultimate pessimist when it came to men. I grew up thinking that all men were terrible and only cared about sex and also that the only way to get a man to like you was to lay down with him. Of course in high school you

have personal development classes where they tell you to abstain until marriage. They were right. But again, it's different hearing it from that person who you trust because they made you and you know they love you. All that I knew about having morals was taught to me in school. But why would I value these lessons if I didn't care what x+2 equals? Math and morals was the same thing to me. I learned it in a classroom so I didn't care about it..."

"I read your blog about growing up fatherless and the impact it has in one's life. It had me in tears and in reflection. As successful as I am now, I walk around looking for validation from men or what my idea of love should be and found myself looking for it in all the wrong men. I didn't grow up with my father and to this day we know each other but as strangers. I am currently working on myself and to love myself but it is a journey that I have to walk alone but I don't want another young girl or boy to look for love from anyone else but from themselves."

Lenyn Mercedes, my mentee of over five years wrote:

"What I needed most was taken from me. All my life I felt neglected and abandoned by my father. It gave me this worthless feeling not having him around, and being told by my grandmother that my dad didn't care about me that he is too busy with his own family. Growing up with my grandmother and her avoidance to talk to me about him as much as I wanted her to. She always avoided these conversations about my father. As a kid I feel you should know what kind of man your father is. What he does for a living, how does he comb his hair, does he like playing catch, is he a family man, does he like dogs or cats, what's his favorite color, what's his favorite smoothie, does he like the power rangers, do we like the same baseball team. Does he get mad if you open the pot before the food is done, crust or no crust on his sandwich? I always wondered. At the age 12

that void was still there, with my unfilled need I asked my grandmother to help me find him. I wanted to meet him but I was nervous that he wouldn't respond or that he would ignore me, I took the chance and after sometime I was able to get in contact with him. He responded and wanted to see me... He wanted to see me! He came and picked me up from my grandmother's house and took me to his home for a few days. We stopped by a clothing store to get me clothes for the week. While we were there he saw that I loved graphic t-shirts and baggy clothes. Immediately he said, 'I'm not buying you any of those clothes'. He picked out a couple button ups and dress pants with the suit jacket. I realized how much I needed this, I was so happy. After that we headed to his house where I met my brothers and sisters on his side of the family, and they welcomed me with open arms. We ate dinner like a family at the table, the first time I ever did that. My questions as a child were being answered without me asking. He asked me did I like smoothies I said yes!! I tried his favorite, it was guava, I didn't like it, he wasn't offended but jokingly told me I had no taste, we were bonding so naturally. At that moment I felt satisfied all at once. This day made all the difference for me... Every kid needs a father."

A father is needed, wanted, craved, and desired. I was fortunate to have several great women that loved me, cared for me, and guided me. I'm very grateful for that. However, I never had a father. I know who my father is, but I cannot recall one time that we had a 'father/son moment' or even a conversation. I missed being taught how to tie a tie or change a tire. I missed out on the 'birds and bees' talk and the discipline and correction from a father that no one believes they want, unless you weren't fortunate enough to experience it, and then you long for a father's discipline.

I was, however, fortunate enough to know it was missing. I knew this because I had friends who had great father/son relationships, relationships that many times made me envious. It allowed me to see the missing ingredient in my life and notice how it impacted me as a person. I had something to compare myself to. I observed how my friends with fathers had more confidence, how they were more social, did better with relationships, and were well-rounded individuals. I saw what I lacked.

Loving fathers positively shape our perception of who we are. A father gives you 'your name,' validates your self-worth, and places that stamp of approval letting you know you have what it takes. In some realities, instead of a father giving their son or daughter their 'name,' the streets are naming them. I was speaking with one of my new mentees and he was explaining to me how he earned his name on the street. He also explained to me some of the things he did that gave him the name he takes so much pride in. He was called, 'Brutal' by the people who knew him because he beat people up - numerous people. He explained that you don't get that name from just a couple fights or from a couple losses. You get it by being vicious to your enemies. Such a title is glorified where he comes from and due to the respect it garnishes, others will look

> A father gives you "your name", validates your self worth, and places that stamp of approval that lets you know you have what it takes.

up to him and want a nickname like that too. Our boys are taking pride in names like 'Hardbody,' 'Savage,' 'Hardhead.' Our girls are taking pride in names like 'Slut,' 'Bitch,' 'Whore.' They're calling each other out of their names with perverse endearment. This happens because they didn't receive the validation of their true identity at home. They never received true titles of honor that inspire them to live up to the best version of themselves.

I had a guest blogger on my website, Brittney LaCour, a young woman who had endured some of the difficult emotional issues that come along with not knowing her identity. She blogged,

"I had boyfriend after boyfriend. I was also what is now called, the side chick...The reason I couldn't keep a guy around was because I needed them. I needed them to validate my existence. I felt better when a guy noticed me and made me feel alive. I didn't have the tools to empower myself, so I searched for validation. I needed them to make me feel important. I always thought that other girls were prettier than me, were smarter than me, and funnier than me."

She didn't know her name, so she searched for her identity and place in the world by attaching herself to shallow relationships. Now when I say name, I'm not talking about the name stamped on her birth certificate. Rather, the name that encourages someone and drives them to succeed, the name that a dad may call his son: *Champ, Prince, Slugger,* or the name he gives to his daughter: *Princess, Baby girl, Doll.* These are names given by a person with loving authority that will always be there for you and constantly reminds you of your worth and potential.

"I was born Reginald Alexander; the inner-city streets christened me "Cash", a nickname that in my younger, misguided years was flaunted and worn like a badge of honor, and one that stood testimonial to my reputation as a big money maker in the illegal drug trade."

This is what happens when the 'oil' is missing in a cake.

One seeks ways to substitute it in the only ways they know how. So the streets become their authority, and the guys who never learned how to be men themselves like the OG who has a criminal record thicker than a dictionary, is where they're learning life's lessons. Thus, they are being exposed to all the things a child should never be exposed to.

It's difficult to determine exactly what we must do to fix the negative authority the streets hold on our young people. We can't find all of their fathers and ensure that they become 'dads' for they themselves may never have learned how to do so. But I've learned that there are substitutes for oil in a cake: Mayonnaise, Apple Sauce, shortening, or pureed fruits. It's not oil but it's good enough to bake a cake. It performs the task of holding the other ingredients together.

You and I can do that. We can't be their biological dad and we'll never be the perfect ingredient, but we can be influential in creating successful young men and young ladies. We can paint the pictures that they desperately need to see. We can be mentors, role models, big brothers, uncles and for many, we will play the role as dad too. It's not 'oil' but it will work!

Painting Pictures Challenge: Fill a void or voids for a young person. So many important experiences are missed for inner-city youth. They need essential guidance, and opportunities to be vulnerable. Allow them to be a kid again and make up for missed moments. This is not just directly for them; it also ensures that they know how to provide these vital moments to their kids. Your effort can impact generations at one time.

CHAPTER 6
THE TEASE

"She dreamed of leaving, but she had too little exposure to the world to imagine where to go."

- Gregory Maguire

O ften times when we go to a sit-down restaurant, we have the opportunity to order appetizers, also known as starters, or at fancy restaurants, hors d'oeuvre. Regardless of what you call it, it's a taste or a sneak preview of what is to come. My favorites are crab cakes, lettuce wraps, chicken wings, or how about some delicious warm spinach artichoke dip. Are you getting hungry yet? We went from baking cakes to eating appetizers. Appetizers are a necessity when you're hungry as they come out much quicker than the entrée; but it serves only as a taste. It really only makes you more hungry, causing you to anticipate the "real meal." If you finish the appetizer and your entrée hasn't hit the table yet it can make one really upset! You feel like you just got teased!

I had the opportunity to bring a group of kids from the inner-city to New York City. It was a great day as we toured the city.

New York was just as I'd hoped it would be for them: fast, lively, and filled with interesting people. The young boys had never seen such organized chaos as people with wild hair, fancy suits, strange piercings, and the like, crossed the busy streets of Manhattan. On avenues where the large stream of New York pedestrians trickled to a manageable crowd, I could see the wonderment on their faces. They took in the sites and cracked jokes at the odd faces they saw and the eccentric performers entertaining for change. It was an eventful day. We visited museums, saw a Broadway play, and ate different foods. An abundance of diverse culture was all around them, hidden in a thousand different niches, waiting to be explored. The day was well spent. Even as night fell, the city stayed the same, hustling and bustling, except they were finally able to witness the bright lights Jay-Z and Alicia Keys made music about. As the trip was coming to an end and as we walked to the train station returning home, one of the young men approached me and said, "You're just teasing me, stop teasing me. You bring me all the way to the city and show me all of this stuff. Then take me back to the hood. I don't want to go back to the hood."

I was shocked. I didn't know what to say. I thought I was doing a good thing. I simply wanted to occupy their idle time so that maybe they wouldn't be getting into trouble. The young man saw it as a tease. In that moment I was honestly hurt because no one likes to be teased and I would in no way be so cruel to vulnerable urban youths. He was right though, I thought. I took him out for a day, *less* than twenty-four hours, showed him a new world and now was dropping him back to his drug infested, poverty stricken, and gang-influenced environment. I'm guilty! I felt horrible; I messed up. Teasing certainly wasn't my intention. Teasing suggests that someone is making fun of you or playing games with your mind. Not what I was trying to do. Then I thought more about it. Horses, donkeys, and mules are teased with a dangling carrot to entice the animal forward. Dolphins are teased with food to perform jaw dropping tricks. Babies are teased with rattles to keep them quiet. Girls tease guys with flirtation to make them earn their affection.

So, when I thought about it in this way, teasing really isn't so bad. The intention of all these situations is to produce something good. The horse wins the race, the dolphin awes the audience, the parent changes the diaper with ease and the guy gets… well you know what he gets. Everyone is happy. So I thought, what's wrong with teasing our inner-city youth if it's going to make them want more than what they are living with daily? Just like the appetizer at the restaurant, the purpose is to tease you and make you hungrier for something more. I find it necessary to provide our youth with appetizers in order to inspire them; teasers that will make them hungry for the many positive opportunities the world has to offer.

The young man exclaimed, "I don't want to go back to the hood!" Later, I understood that this comment suggested I did my job. The fact that he didn't want to go back means that he saw something he liked better. He saw something that if he had the opportunity to achieve, he would pursue. He saw something that didn't look like his environment but maybe reminded him of his childhood dreams. So in that moment, I understood my mission. My mission is to expose or 'tease' inner-city youth and bring them to the point of awareness that they can have so much more.

As a young woman on her way to adulthood, Oprah was made aware of all she could become. We learn that she was exposed to reading at the age of 3, already reading and writing when she entered kindergarten at the age of 5. She acknowledges that teachers and schools showed her the way out. Her awareness was pivotal to her success.

Our youth lack this kind of awareness. The young person that says I want to stay in the projects, run the streets all my life, and die like a man is the young person who isn't aware of their own potential mainly because they haven't seen anything else. Those with such ideals have a narrow view because of their lack of exposure. Often times we feel like these are the types of kids you can't take anywhere because they won't appreciate it, or they won't know how to behave, or maybe that won't get it. I disagree, these are the kids that you take everywhere so that they learn how to appreciate it, learn new behaviors, and get the understanding that the world is theirs – the whole wide world. They can climb Mt. Everest, or take a picture on the Colorado Rockies, walk across the London Bridge. They can be international travelers, work for major corporations, and live their childhood dreams. I was always taught, "You learn better, you do better." However, learning involves teaching. That's where you and I come in.

I remember taking my first flight to California. The experience of boarding the plane and arriving to another state across the country on the same day at almost the same time because of the time zone change was amazing. Also experiencing a new location that looked different, where the climate was different, the people dressed different, and their vernacular was different, was a big eye opener! It was the beginning of my realization that the world is very big.

I grew up sheltered and hardly made it out of a 10 mile radius of my home. So on many levels I never knew what was beyond my school, church, and the community park. I only knew what I saw, which meant my perspective of the world was small. When I finally got out of the state and saw something beyond my neighborhood, I was in awe. I started traveling more because that experience changed my life; I just wanted to see more. So, I started looking for reasons to travel, and I met some family that I didn't know growing up. They lived in Colorado, and we developed a relationship as I began visiting them every few months. Sitting on the mountains and seeing the vastness of the world, driving through town and seeing all the open land, visiting the tourist locations like The Garden of the Gods and Colorado's North Pole Santa's Workshop are moments that I won't forget. They broadened my understanding. These trips whet my appetite and now fifteen years later, I've been to Texas, North

Carolina, South Carolina, New Orleans, Mississippi, Oklahoma, Maryland, Pennsylvania, New York, Georgia, Alabama, Delaware, Florida, Virginia, New Hampshire, Mexico, Israel, Bahamas, Costa Rica, London, Spain, and I have so much more to see.

Anytime you see something out of your familiar realm and beyond what you know, it creates a new worldview. Your perspective is limited to what you see. We all have different opinions on various matters because of our different experiences and levels of exposure. Our youth who have only seen street life can only see through that lens but those who have seen something greater and bigger than their neighborhoods, although they are still living in them, will know that there's more to life than what meets the eye.

In photography, the exposure of film to light results in a photograph. The same applies in the lives of our young people. Exposing them to light, to the world, to the arts, new people, new opportunities, new situations, new places, art or music, and opportunities to observe the accomplishments of others will paint new pictures for them. It will create the photograph.

"You can only aspire to the level of your awareness and exposure. Your exposure helps you to dream. You can never dream of something you have never come across. It is important to take note of the areas that increase your level of exposure as that becomes the much needed arsenal to propel you to the next level of life. I recall a conversation I held with two kids whose mothers were maids or home assistants. They were both about 4 years old. I asked a simple question, "What do you want to do when you are grown up?" Their answers were bold and to the point. "To be a home assistant; maid". It proved to me that because their exposure level was low, they felt this was the career to choose." (Shumba).

We talk about the need for our kids to beat the statistics, overcome the barriers of their neighborhoods and become successful, but how can we want this if we aren't willing to show them what that looks like, what the world looks like, or what success looks like? A tease could save a child's life. The difference between those who become a product of their environment and those who do not is because they had a glimpse of something better. They were provided opportunities to grow.

Leadership trainer and speaker Alexander Den Heijer said, "When a flower doesn't bloom you fix the environment in which it grows, not the flower." We are so quick to say that there's something wrong with today's youth. We say that they don't have the right outlook, motivation, or skills to succeed. The youth are the flowers that Den Heijer talks about. There's nothing wrong with the flower, it just needs to be positioned in the right environment to grow, an environment that provides the necessary exposure.

> There's nothing wrong with the flower, it just needs to be positioned in the right environment to grow, an environment that provides the necessary exposure.

My friend, Elijah, grew up in the DYFS system. All his life he moved from home to home. When he became a teenager, he found himself homeless as not many families or would-be parents desire to take in teenagers. People see teenagers as too great of a risk. He talks about how these moments pushed him to bad decision making, drug addiction, and incarceration. The only thing he had going for him was an incredible ability to play football. He says the only reason he survived was because he saw glimpses of a better life. He saw these glimpses as sports created opportunities to travel with his team and see new communities with bleachers filled with family and friends supporting the home team. He saw elaborate marching bands and remembers a particular band at West Essex where the conductor of the marching band stood on a 15 foot ladder and conducted the whole band during the national anthem opening song. This was quite different from what he saw at the home games which consisted of barely 4 drums, unskilled cheerleaders with no uniforms, and only a few parents in attendance. If he was limited to what he saw at home and in his community, he attests that he would have remained there, perhaps becoming a statistic of unemployment, violence, or drug activity.

These glimpses of outside communities saved his life.

I've heard many others say things like, "sports saved my life," "music saved my life," "after school clubs saved my life," "summer camp saved my life," "church saved my life." The reason why people say this and what they all have in common is that they provide new experiences and exposure for a young person.

In the 2007 film, *Freedom Writers*, we find a white, female teacher going into a classroom, where most of her students were African-American and Latino teenagers from Long Beach, California. These students were considered 'unteachable,' and the expectation of the school administration was very low for them. The school didn't invest in this group of students since they had been written off as dropouts, baby mamas, thugs, and gangsters. Their teacher, played by actress Hilary Swank, attempts to provide instruction and because the school didn't make the investment, she chooses to make the investment herself and takes on two part-time jobs to purchase new text books. She exposes her class of misfits and marginalized teens to poetry, she invited holocaust survivors to speak, and she had the women who sheltered Anne Frank lecture the class. She exposed them to a new world and with great opposition took them to the Museum of Tolerance. Exposure was the key to success in her classroom. This film shows a teacher that opened the eyes of inner-city youth. The movie ends with a note stating that many successfully graduated and went to college. We, the audience, are convinced that their success is attributed to their teacher's investment and effort to provide these students with new experiences.

I've experienced many amazing moments and memories with youths from the inner-city, but I'll never forget when I chaperoned a trip to an Amusement Park with a group of youth that were in a detention alternative program. They were heavily gang influenced and had juvenile criminal records. This trip both changed their worldview and my perspective of them. The same kids that are 'too cool for school' and have street names that depict a badass mentality become the silliest kids at the amusement park. They rode baby rides and were on the tea cups because they were too scared to get on the big roller coasters. Not to mention they had the widest grins on their faces and were running around as if they had never seen anything like it, primarily because they had not. They were teenagers just a year or two from being adults but had never been to an amusement park. They never had the opportunity to be kids because their environment sucked them in and the system was too busy locking them up. So, rather than getting glimpses of success, they got frequent glimpses of detention centers, group homes, and restricted programming.

"Each year it is estimated that approximately 500,000 youth are brought to juvenile detention centers. On any given day more than 26,000 youth are detained… 70 percent are detained for nonviolent offenses." (Holman and Ziedenberg).

Detention centers have their place, but too often they create more problems than solutions. Detention centers create more negative relationships, more bad habits, and more gang affiliations as they are surrounded with youth similar to them, going down the same path and perhaps leading them to worse. However, the system also considers Juvenile Detention Centers to be a 'tease'. Detention Centers are meant to be a tease to strike fear in the hearts of youth not to reoffend or age out and end up in adult jail. We spend a lot of money to put fear in the hearts of youth with scared straight programs, but it's not working. The recidivism rates are devastating!

San Jose Police Chief Bill Lansdowne said, "Locking up kids is the easiest way. But once they get in the juvenile justice system, it's very hard to get them out."

Our inner-city youth become familiar with being locked up, so it's no longer a big deal. It's like constantly beating a child for misbehaving. At some point this style of discipline is ineffective as it becomes routine. As Chief Landsdowne said, "it's the easiest way." Detaining youth is easier than making an investment to help shape them through good counsel, mentorship, and opportunities. Society is more willing to spend an average of $652.15 per day to detain a youth rather than investing these dollars into programming that will 'tease' them to become better citizens.

Shame on us!

I'm an advocate for youth programs that help redirect youth to make better decisions, taking time to expose them to an alternative way of life. Our young people need glimpses of college, for many of them have never visited a college campus. They need exposure to young people striving for success. Young black boys and black girls, in addition to other minority groups in the inner-city need exposure to new cultures and food by being exposed to fine dining restaurants. They need the opportunity to dress up for a celebratory event to help them understand the importance of an encouraging presentation. African-American youth need glimpses of healthy relationships to better understand what a nuclear family looks like and what type of family goals they can have for themselves. Even travel, they need exposure to the world, new cities, states, and countries. They need to see the geographic possibilities. If their environment is the biggest culprit, let's show them new environments.

> If their environment is the biggest culprit, let's show them new environments.

If we are to reverse the curse of the outcome of bad environments, we must do so by doing the opposite - exposing them to healthy environments. Some may question whether we are rewarding bad behavior. No, we're providing what's most needed to create desire in the hearts of youth. Without desire, contentment is present. Let's dangle the carrot before them (teasing them) until they run after it.

Painting Pictures Challenge: Propel youth to want more by showing them more. Seek to discover what they haven't experienced and give them that. Don't limit your time with them to their neighborhoods. There's a big world out there so show them a little each time. Also, introduce them to people that aren't like them, who look different, act different, and think differently.

This too is a way to show them the world.

CHAPTER 7
ESCAPING

"The difficulty lies not so much in developing new ideas as in escaping from old ones."

- John Maynard Keynes

Have you ever played the "claw game" at an arcade? The game where you operate a crane like controller to win a prize. It seems like it's up to you to win, but the game really doesn't allow many to win. The controls are clunky, the claw doesn't close all the way, and all the expensive items are stuck at the bottom (but you aren't told this before you put your money in). The game is designed for you to fail because if everybody won, too many iPods, iPads, and hundred dollar bills would be given out. I've tried plenty of times, wasted lots of money and could not win these great prizes. It seems so easy, all you have to do is secure the prize in the 'claws' and move it to the location where it will drop in the shoot and you win! But getting the prize into the shoot is rarely done. It's an impossible possibility.

It's not as easy as it sounds for inner-city youth to begin a new journey even after being exposed to something better. As the young man reminded me, "I have to go back to the hood." Going back to the hood means so much more than him having to eat and sleep there. It also means that he's going back to a place of captivity, a place that wants to hold him down. "I was created to fail; I just can't win," one young man told me.

Sadly many young people can't get out of the 'hood' because of parents and family who intentionally or neglectfully hold them down. We see it all the time: parents who burden their children with 'grown up' responsibilities and little attention to academic success, parents that validate the misbehaviors of their child by telling the teacher off at school, parents who discharge their child from valuable programming because they don't like someone.

One young man I worked with in a detention alternative program had completed the program successfully but continued to come week after week. He was thirsty for the valuable information provided. He wanted to do better, so he was voluntarily putting himself in environments where he could improve his life. He eventually became transparent about situations at home and his community and was asking for assistance, but before I knew it he was gone. He no longer showed up after being the first to every meeting over the past several months. I didn't think anything of it at first but after several missed meetings, I phoned his home and his mother told me, "I don't want you or this program in our business. My son is fine; I don't need anybody to help me raise my son." I hung up the phone with a heavy heart for a kid who wanted to get out, but couldn't.

It's the Crab Bucket Effect. If one crab attempts to escape from a bucket of live crabs, the others will pull it back down rather than allow it to be free. And because a crab doesn't have quick speed, as most of its life has been spent buried under sand, it can never get out quick enough.

Our young people have difficulties getting out because like the crab, they don't have quick speed. I think their speed has been impeded not only by family members but by their own 'double desires.' They've seen better and they want out, but they also are more familiar with living inside the bucket rather than the vast and unfamiliar possibilities outside of the bucket. And while they enjoy and welcome new experiences, it still isn't totally believable or attainable to them.

I can understand this. I often find myself wanting something, but become snagged upon some great sense of unfamiliarity which equals great risk. So, the thought becomes, 'do I choose to be complacent and remain with the life I know, or dream and fight for what "could" be better?' Someone once said, "The known devil is better than the unknown angel." So, for our young people, if they feel like they were born in the bucket and they've survived this long in the same environment, why change it for some unknown possibilities?

It's called the mere-exposure effect which causes one to develop a preference for things simply because it's more familiar. Whether it's better or not, familiarity breeds contentment.

One evening a young man called me in distress. He was crying uncontrollably. "It's hard!" he cried. I'm trying to make the right choices and do the right thing but "It's Hard." I just advocated for this young man in court a few weeks prior as the plan was to send him away for two years. He just recently had a newborn and he, his mom, and I, in desperation, pleaded with the judge to give him another chance. This young man in all sincerity said to the judge, "I need to be there for my daughter. I will do whatever I have to." I have every belief that he meant these words – it wasn't an act. But just a few weeks later he called me to say, "I can't do it. I know what I promised, but it's too hard." He said, "We don't have any money, my baby has no clothes, I wear the same thing every day and now its winter. I'm cold and my family and I are hungry. I can't do this." He said, "I never wanted for anything. I always had the money to do what I needed. I have to go back to doing what I know, selling drugs." I heard him loud and clear. I get it, it's hard, but it's worth it, I said. I didn't know what else to say, he was hurting so badly. At that moment, I told him to meet me at my office, I took him to get groceries, picked up some clothes for the kid, completed job applications and I encouraged him to hang in there. The next week, he started a job at UPS and things were on the up and up. Again, he calls me in desperation, "I can't do this. Yeah I have a job, but it's not the kind of money I'm used to." Within the next few days, I receive a call that he's been locked up again, but this time he's 18 and the consequences are much more severe.

This young man wanted to achieve, as do many. The fact that he kept calling me, talking it out with tears flowing says to me that he wanted it badly. He could have easily gone ahead and did what he knew best, but he called for help because he really wanted to get out. His brain was steering him to do the familiar.

I've seen the desire on the face of many other young people. I've witnessed moments during group sessions where a kid gets it, moments when improvements become real and I could see that kid making strides to get out of the bucket. These youths have even gone as far as saying, "I can't do this no more, I can't be the next one, I don't want to hurt my moms, I'm done with it." I've seen tears in their eyes as I had tears in my eyes, the moments are very much real.

In my many visits to kids in detention centers, they've assured me that this was the last time; they were going to do the right thing, finish school and make everyone proud. In moments like those, they are attempting to climb out. Unfortunately, these moments often fade. I've watched them fade right after a young person conveys an excellent plan, then ends with I'm going to 'try' my best. You can watch the battle in their mind as they repeat it softly to themselves, as if they're trying to convince themselves as well.

It becomes a battle in their minds between reality and fantasy, between the genuine optimism of how life can be and then the heavy reality of how things currently are. They want to believe they can do better, but the image of their realities says otherwise. Young men struggling to turn away from

> It becomes a conflict in their minds between reality and fantasy.

the fast life of dealing drugs have become accustomed to having money and making it in their own way, so it becomes difficult to adjust to a new way of earning money without the basic means of living. They might have even taken a liking to the popularity and status they've attained, and how can they risk losing that? They've enjoyed the recognition, so who would desire to give that up? Even more, their mind, so invested in the lifestyle of the streets, says that this new life, clean and honest, isn't you. Considering all they've seen and been exposed to, a new life seems like nothing more than a fairy tale. It's the kind of fairy tale that's been told so often you already know the ending: predictable but unrealistic. It's like Cinderella escaping the mistreatment of her evil step mother, Sleeping Beauty escaping her death curse with a kiss from the prince, or Snow White also escaping a curse and being awakened. Or maybe it's more like the three little pigs escaping the destruction of the big bad wolf. Simba escaping the hyenas that were meant to kill him, but of course, they all 'live happily ever after.'

I've come to understand that the reason why every good fairy tale, every great blockbuster movie, and every remarkable theatrical production has a plot that involves escaping the bad guy is because that's what we love to see. We love to hear about it because that's what we all want for ourselves in different areas.

Late British journalist, essayist and businessman Walter Bagehot said, "All the best stories in the world are but one story in reality, the story of escape. It is the only thing which interests us all and at all times, how to escape."

Our young people want to escape too and 'live happily ever after.' They want to sit in a big 'boss' chair (It's incredible how youth that I mentor will sit in my chair and feel a sense of pride), have an office with a window, have the power to hire and fire. They want an honest life, they want to escape, but it's so hard for them. The fairy tale that we 'tease' them with seems unlikely.

Unfortunately, it's more complicated for some than it is for others. Some have become so engulfed that they are slaves to the streets. I saw a discouraging social media post that read,

I will kidnap you, raise you, and return you to your family so they can bury you.
Sincerely,
The Streets

This was grave but so true. It just seems that our black youth are held captive by the streets. Families will see their sons, daughters, nieces, and nephews grow up, playing games of hide and seek, freeze tag, man hunt as every kid should. Sadly, once the streets grab hold of them they may never really see them again, except lying in a casket. Parents have told me that they don't ever see their son or daughter. They may come home and change clothes and be gone for weeks. They don't even know who they are anymore. The streets are aggressive and are kidnapping our youth with too much on the line for them to get out.

A youth gang survey analysis conducted by the National Gang

Center captured the devastating effects of gangs on the lives of inner-city youth. The most recent estimates state there are more than 30,000 gangs and about 850,000 gang members nationally.

This signifies that gangs are a major culprit of misguided teens. The greater problem is that gangs are known to be easy to enter but hard as hell to exit.

"I know a few people that died trying to get out," said a 19-year-old Chicagoan who used to be a member of the "governing board" of a major West Side Chicago gang.

"As far as I'm concerned, I'm no longer in this gang, but they don't know that," said the young man, who asked that his name not be used. "If you tell them, 'I don't want to be in the gang' and stuff, they cut your tattoos off your arm. They beat you in the head with a baseball bat." (Johnson and Thomas).

It has been said that the young man I spoke of earlier, who was shot directly in the head, was on his way to break ties with the street when he became a victim of gun violence. He was on his way to hand in his street card, denounce that life, and start a new journey. He had shared that desire with me days before; he was tired of the street life. I was so proud of his decision, but the streets didn't let him. The streets would rather see him dead than progress in life.

As we consider the crab bucket effect again, think about it like this: every crab knows their ultimate destiny is to be dropped in a pot of boiling water. But instead of pushing up the crab that's trying to get out, the crabs in the bucket will pull him back down so they all die together. This is what's happening in our neighborhoods.

In the book entitled "Into The Abyss: A Personal Journey into the World of Street Gangs," Dr. Mike Carlie writes "A juvenile officer who works with juvenile gang members told me a story about a local gang member who wanted to get out of his gang. "I got a call from a client named Fernando," she said, "who told me he needed help. He was frightened ... he didn't want to be in the gang anymore. As far as the officer was concerned, he was in too far. I didn't think he could get out. He actually wanted me to lock him up so that he'd stay out of trouble." The officer told her client she couldn't do that, so he broke into a car, stole some things, assaulted his parents and another youth then fled. He wanted to get locked up, and since I wouldn't do that, he tried doing some things he could get locked up for. Another of her gang clients told her, "I'm going to kill him," referring to the young man who wanted to leave the gang. "He can't leave."

This story confirms the notion that many gang affiliated youths want out. They don't want to continue the cycle of criminal activity and violence but have been convinced and intimidated into believing they can't leave. The streets invoke a fear to stay and a fear to remain loyal. It's almost as if they belong to the streets – well at least that's what the block has taught them. Their brains have been infiltrated

> Their brains have been infiltrated to believe that they are the property of their hood-sworn to allegiance.

to believe that they are the property of their hood – sworn to allegiance.

One evening, I ran a group session and it was more unusual than normal. The participants who were usually engaged and responsive were on edge and defiant. I didn't know what was going on. I thought maybe they just weren't responding well to the topic of the evening. Shortly after, I received a call from the detention center sergeant and he explained to me that it was gang initiation night and many of these young people were both anxious and fearful about what was about to happen. Many of them had to do things that they didn't want to do. They had become slaves to the streets and while they would prefer not to do it; they found themselves trapped.

Dr. Carlie also writes:

A gang enforcement officer and national trainer told me that if "... a Hispanic gang member wishes to get out of his gang, some gangs will allow this to occur. Others will not. Some of them require membership for life. When getting out is allowed, it might be done in some cruel ways. It might be through being jumped out, where they beat up the person trying to leave; through being cut out, where they stab him and if he survives, he's out and if he dies he's out; or he might be boxed out. Being boxed out means he's placed in an old refrigerator that's been laid on the ground, the door is shut and the other gang members gather around the refrigerator and usually fire five rounds into it with a twenty-two caliber pistol. If the gang member in the box survives, he's out and if he dies, he's out."

I reflect back on the idea of a fairy tale and ask myself every day, why must a happy ending be so difficult to achieve in the streets? Why can't there be mistakes and still room for 'do overs' or forgiveness?

Our youth have entered a building believing it was safe for it provided the support they needed and the acknowledgement they craved. No, the building certainly was no mansion or fancy apartment. The doormen in the lobby wore tattoos and gang colors instead of an elaborate uniform; the elevators never worked because, well, what's the sense in repairing it? There were no authorities responding to distress calls from this area. Still the building provided more support and shelter than the wild lawlessness of the streets. It even put a band aid on the pain the inhabitants experienced, since they all came from the same place. Now, since the building had never promised safety, it is on fire and the youth wants to get out. It's smoky and the youth can't breathe. They're gagging, gasping for air, and are in a frantic desperation to flee. They feel trapped, and they can't find the door that will provide the possibility of an exit. There's no way out, they believe, so they resign themselves to death not realizing that every building is required to have a fire escape, even one as broken and cruel as this. An escape plan is posted in every hallway, in every apartment. "EXIT!" it exclaims in great red letters. When the youth recalls this, he or she crawls under the smoke, as instincts would tell them to, and fumble through the dark to find the fire escape. With a lot of effort and much risk, they make their way down the ladder one step at a time, still reeling from the effects of the fumes. Perhaps the effects are too great and some fall off the ladder and die trying to escape, while others make it all the way down and find safety. So while the fire escape didn't save them all, it did save some.

You and I must be the fire escape. Although all won't escape, many will because of the support that we provide. A fire escape is made of steel and built to support a lot of weight. I hope you too feel like you are built or created to provide support to marginalized youth who have found themselves stuck in a burning building. While escaping isn't easy, it is possible.

Painting Pictures Challenge: Escaping is hard. Acknowledge to your youth that you understand how difficult it is. I challenge you to share a personal story of a time when you couldn't escape. We've all felt trapped at some time in life. Transparency is vital to a great mentoring relationship. Talk about your experience and its outcome (whether good or bad), be honest. Let them know you believe that when they're truly ready, they will make that great escape, and you will be there to support them.

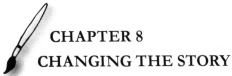

CHAPTER 8
CHANGING THE STORY

"I think back on a childhood full of longing to belong and I see my life now as what I have created from my dreams. An image comes to mind of Mrs. Brown at the orphanage in Cleveland, me sitting at her side, telling her, "You'll read about me someday."

- Antwone Fisher

Our youth are experiencing a fire that is meant to kill them. The fire is hotter than it was for their parents, grandparents, or great grandparents. Every generation has greater challenges, temptations, and peer pressure than the generations before them.

For that reason, the fire has killed too many and many others have become victims of the fire's residue. However, a life of hope and purpose can be obtained after a difficult upbringing, after being in and out detention centers, after being a victim to the streets. One can still emerge strong, ambitious, and successful.

Lupita Nyong'o said, "No matter where you're from, your dreams are valid," I agree, but I would like to add my own twist, "No matter what you did, your dreams are valid."

This past summer I met a young man while at a campground

with some inner-city youth. He was one of the camp counselors. He was conducting outdoor activities with a group of young people, and I was observing from a distance. It was the first day and they were all getting to know each other, so they were playing one of my favorite games, Two Truths and a Lie. It was his turn, (the camp counselor) and he said, "My name is Christopher, I belonged to a gang, and I'm a college basketball player." This was an easy one, as I'm participating from a distance. The lie is obvious, he's definitely never been in a gang, I said to myself. The young people were on the same page as they guessed first that he was not gang involved. When he said nope that's the truth, I was shocked and interrupted the game to talk to him. I'm not sure what he thought at that moment. Did he think I wouldn't want him to work with the youth because of his past? I hope not, for I wanted to talk to him because I found it to be amazing what he has become.

I'm always intrigued by success stories: they inspire, motivate, and propel me toward my mission. That evening we talked and this young man, Christian Filpo and not Christopher, which turned out to be the lie, began to explain to me how he joined the gang when he was 13 years old, in the 8th grade. He found himself getting into fights and selling drugs. He conveyed the struggle of growing up, born and bred in Washington Heights, experiencing homelessness and having to live in a shelter. He talked about everything he saw, the drugs, violence, and tragedy. He spoke of his unforgettable experience when two boys from his school and his older cousin took him to a vacated apartment and, 'scared shitless,' he is exposed to machetes and other various weapons. He said, "For that three hour meeting in a vacated apartment in Harlem, I felt like God told me I was going down the wrong path… funny part is I'm not religious. I've been inside a church maybe twice."

He also shared with me the story of his escape. He said, "I had a vision that many of my peers didn't have. Once I didn't want to live that lifestyle anymore, I completely separated myself from the 'homies.' He didn't allow his past to determine his future. But because I know escaping isn't the easiest thing to do, I asked him how? He said, escaping is in my blood, and he began to explain an incredible story of how his mother had to escape from the Dominican Republic:

He said, "During the 1980s, my mother desired to be an independent woman and the idea to migrate emerged when she could not continue on to college. One of twelve children in her family, she had neither financial support nor transportation abilities and it impeded her in finishing her education. She sneaked away from home thinking that receiving a Visa to the U.S. as a Temporary Visitor with limited documents would be easy. Unfortunately, her Visa request was negated. Trying to keep her intentions in migrating secretive, she could not go back home to get the proper documentation needed to complete the process. All she had with her were school papers and her father's documentation. When she did come back home, her father became aware of her intentions. He kicked her out of the house; she became abandoned by her family. At this point, her hopes in migrating to America were reignited."

He continued to say, "She received false papers from family friends and decided to migrate illegally with her sister's ex-husband. She vividly remembered trembling on the passenger seat from how nervous she was for traveling with a different identity." He spoke of how his mother met a Puerto Rican man in New York, who was directly a second-class U.S. citizen as a result of the America's imperial objectives. "They agreed to marry for $5,000 and soon became a victim for ransom. When she received her appointment to become a permanent resident, the Puerto Rican man had disappeared with her money. So when immigration detectives went to investigate her case and realized that her "husband" was not present in her life, my mother was imprisoned for three days in the Dominican Republic. Once she was released, she attempted to go back home forgivingly, but was not accepted by her family. She desperately needed to go back to her new home in New York. Her best friend helped her gain access to legitimate documentation with her personal information to travel. Since she was deported, connections were made for her to fly from the Dominican Republic to Panama, from Panama to Mexico, crossing the border to San Diego, and from San Diego to New York. This in itself exemplifies the miserable conditions my mother was living in. Abandoned and desperate, she decided to take the risk. In Panama, she was kidnapped and held hostage by men and was sent to Mexico. Her desire of experiencing the American dream was again deterred. The traumatic events she experienced throughout Central America to come back to her American home were devastating." He then said, "It's in my blood… escaping is in my blood."

This young man is now attending Trinity College on a scholarship, studying abroad in Trinidad and Tobago, double majoring in Sociology and International Studies focusing on Latin America and the Caribbean. His future goal is to make a difference for young kids living in urban areas.

This young man is a demonstration that you can change your story. He reminded me that the fire doesn't have to burn you. I was surprised by his past because, he didn't look like his story, and he didn't look like his bad experiences. I heard a quote that said, "Those with the greatest futures are those with the worst past."

This is true when we consider people like D.L. Hughley, Nick Cannon, and Mark Wahlberg.

D.L. Hughley, one of the great stand-up comedians of our day, grew up in Los Angeles where he was affiliated with the Bloods gang and was always in trouble. He changed the story.

Nick Cannon, a man of many talents, grew up in a neighborhood near San Diego and also became associated with the Bloods gang. He saw his friends shot and killed and he changed the story for himself.

Mark Wahlberg, one of the highest paid actors, struggled with drug use, was gang affiliated and at 16 years old was looking at some serious time with an attempted murder charge. He changed the story.

In the Antwone Fisher movie, a true story, he had many traumatic experiences as I stated earlier, but his foster mother, Ms. Tate, also constantly destroyed the potential of a positive future orientation for him. "I don't know which one of you no-good, rotten, hardheaded niggas put your dirty hands on my walls... I took you in when your no good mammies threw you away..." These words could have destroyed him, but he changed the story.

The quote that began this chapter has a powerful message. He said, "You're going to read about me someday," not because he had committed a murder or was killed himself, but because he made something of himself. Years later he came back to tell Ms. Tate, "It don't matter what you tried to do, you couldn't destroy me! I'm still standing! I'm still strong! And I always will be."

The real Antwone Fisher has become a great screenwriter and producer, receiving the renowned Humanities Prize, The Screenwriter of the year award from the National Association of Theater Owners, and was listed in Variety's "Fifty People to Watch." His promise to Ms. Tate came true.

Our youth can change the story too. No matter what they did, no matter how many bad choices they made. We must help them create a positive future orientation and that is to change their thoughts, plans, motivations, hopes and feelings about their future. We talked earlier about how environmental factors have limited their ability to have hope for their destinies, this is why they have such a negative view on the future. Why attend school if the story says they are more likely to end up in jail than graduate? Why strive to do well, if the

> Our youth can change the story too.

story says they won't live past thirty? Why try if the story says no one cares? Why apply to college if the story says you aren't college material?

The stories that our youth hear and see have created a destructive mind set, one of gloom and doom. I've gone into high schools and heard guidance counselors say, "These students can't get into any university." I've heard stories of teachers say, "you will never be able to obtain that dream, it's too ambitious," "What's wrong with you, everyone else gets it," "I get paid whether you succeed or not." These words are fatal and too often become their stories. They create stories of low achievement, failure, and negativity. I remember that old children's rhyme, "Sticks and stones will break my bones, but words will never hurt me." I disagree with that, words from adults have pushed our youth to gangs, drug addictions, and hopelessness.

It is important to note however, studies have shown that we can change the stories of our youth with positive future orientation. A study conducted with 850 teens from at-risk high schools found that "positive future orientation" was directly related to lower levels of violence in teens. Findings suggest that interventions that foster the development of future goals and aspirations for young people could play a vital role in violence prevention efforts. "These interventions could help youth develop a sense of hope in their future by providing experiences that assist them to see the possibilities for themselves." (Sarah Stoddard)

I enjoy Ted Talks and I recall one presentation entitled,

"Everyone needs a Champion." It's quite humorous, but has some great truth as well. The speaker, Ms. Pierson, a teacher for forty years, tells a story and says, "I gave a quiz – twenty questions and the student missed eighteen. I put a + 2 on his paper, he came and asked me, 'Ms. Pierson is this an F?' – I said 'Yes,' he said, 'then why did you put a smiley face on it'... I said, 'Cause you're on the road. You got two right; you didn't miss them all... eighteen sucks all the life out of you, + 2 says I'm not all bad."

This story is a demonstration of how to create a positive future orientation. It creates a desire for a young person to work harder and desire more and changes their outlook. It reminds them that they're "not all bad." It encourages them to understand that a failure doesn't exclude them from great achievement. How can we do this daily with our young people? How do we restructure the future orientation of our youth, which ultimately changes their story? Big problems don't always require big solutions. Here are ten intervention strategies that I have found effective, but simple:

1. Care, Care, Genuinely care – One of the greatest ways to gain the attention of a young person is to care for them. Make every effort to acknowledge them and remember something they told you in prior conversations (even when they act like they don't care.) Your care is best revealed to a young person through persistence.

2. Patience – Allow them to make mistakes but don't allow their mistakes to change your interactions or your persistence.

Celebrate the small successes – it may take a long time to see substantial change.

3. Listen – Hear them when they're talking *and* when they aren't. Take note of their non-verbal cues. Acknowledge what you hear and how their thoughts are important.

4. Help them Set Goals – The b clause to this strategy is "be realistic." Setting realistic goals are key to adopting any new behavior. Lofty goals will cause both them and you to feel defeated if they are not accomplished.

5. Understand- Youth long for adults who are willing to understand them and who will provide the acceptance and guidance they need without judgment.

6. Be a Motivator and Encourager – Everyone wants to know that they have what it takes because it becomes fuel for them to run on. Make sure they know that you believe in them and *really do* believe in them!

7. Be a Great Role Model – Lead by example and show them the way. Don't do what you encourage them not to do.

8. Ask them about the positive events of their day or week – I start every conversation by asking, "what's good?" Not to be cool, but rather to inquire of the positive happenings of the week. Sure, I'll listen to the negative too, but I strive to create a positive thinking mindset.

9. Stay involved – Be consistent, be available, be present.

10. Give them Exposure – Show them a life they've never seen before. Create new positive desires for them.

Without intervention, the story will be difficult to change because in order to change the story, a new outlook is required. We can be instrumental in changing the outlook.

> Without intervention, the story will be difficult to change.

The stories of success mentioned earlier don't have to be exceptions. Some might say D.L. Hughley, Nick Cannon, Mark Wahlberg and maybe the camp counselor story are all miracles and not every day occurrences. However, I believe they can be everyday occurrences, escaping and changing the story *can* become the norm. The statistics can change mightily only if you and I make the required investment.

There's a story in the Bible about three teenagers who were thrown into a furnace that was meant to kill them and this furnace was heated seven times more than its normal temperature. The fire was so hot that it killed the soldiers that threw them in. There was no escape, and they were trapped with death being their only option. The story ends like this: they came out, and escaped the fire unharmed, without even the stench of fire.

Everyone expected them not to survive, but they changed the story. I trust that this will be the case for our marginalized youth. This can be the story of those who said they could never amount to anything, could never become successful, and could never live a long, fulfilling life. I believe that these stories will be changed insomuch that it will shock the entire world! The world needs this kind of shock!

Painting Pictures Challenge: Believe in our youth and let them know that you trust them. I will often intentionally do things to show my mentees that I trust them by giving them my car keys to grab something out of the car or trusting them with cash to get something from the store. It has never backfired on me. I believe that if you show them that you believe in the possibility of them changing their story, they won't let you down. Believing in them goes along way!

CHAPTER 9
PAINTING PICTURES

"I am only one. But still I am one. I cannot do everything, but still I can do something. Because I cannot do everything, I will not refuse to do the something that I can do."

- Edward Everett Hale

Most of this book was written while I was in the mountains of Vermont. While this location is peaceful and beautiful with scenes of untouched life and nature, one must climb many hills to see the most spectacular view. One evening just before the sun fell below the hills and the pine trees in the west, I decided to climb. It was my last night in Vermont and I wanted to see the view as the sun set that evening. I climbed swiftly although not very well prepared. I didn't have the right shoes, I didn't pack any water and I had no flashlight, but I climbed. Dusk fell quickly in the mountains and I was not willing to travel back to the cabin so soon, so I kept pace avoiding that scenario. At some moments I rested because I felt out of breath and the hill became so steep at some parts that it seemed as if I were crawling on my hands and feet more than I walked. My legs became tired, and I heard rustling in the woods that could have been any number of wild animals prepared to attack. A mother bear in the woods of Vermont was more likely than I would have cared to consider, for it certainly wasn't far-fetched. I was alone, so I was alert to the possibility that I could be attacked. Fear gripped my heart and I began to turn around a few times. Every time I thought to retreat back to my cabin, I imagined the amazing picture I could take on the summit of this mountain. I thought of how the view would be amazing, just picture perfect. Finally, I got to the top and watched in awe as the sun sunk into the horizon. I took many pictures to remember the moment before heading back down. I was glad I didn't give up. This was another amazing moment that I would never forget but it took work, dedication, and discipline.

We all want to see a brighter future for this generation, but it's going to be a journey, a hike, similar to a mountain climb for us to see the manifestation of a brighter future. It's going to take work, dedication, and discipline on our part to not give up on the picture that is waiting to be seen, the purpose that is undiscovered and the potential that needs to be cultivated.

It's going to take time! It's a great challenge and I attest to that. However, we must go in understanding that these young people didn't become rambunctious and rebellious overnight. For some it has been years of molestation, years of watching mom have a new boyfriend every week, years of witnessing gun violence, years of losing loved ones to the streets, and years of having to fend for themselves. It took time for them to get where they are and I can guarantee it will take time to get out of it.

I've had the opportunity to supervise youth advocates and while many of them had a passion for young people and seeing them embark on their purpose, some didn't realize how much investment has to be made before a return is seen. So during moments of supervision, I would hear advocates say things like, "I can't get through, he's not changing" or "I think she's getting worse." I would respond by asking a series of questions:

How long have you been working with them?

Are they attending school?

Were they attending school when you began mentoring them?

Have they been making better decisions?

Often times the responses to the above questions helps them to understand that something is happening. Perhaps, the youth wasn't in school when they began the program and now they are attending 3 days a week. While they still have anger issues, they are less frequent. While they still have bad peer associations, they are also creating more positive relationships. They were once unengaging, but now they have moments of opening up and vulnerability. And while the improvements are inconsistent, nonetheless, improvements are being made. Many young people we come across are like a bank account in a severe deficit. So, while deposits are being made, it's going to take a while to get it out of the red. With short strokes, a better picture is being painted.

Remember, Picasso didn't paint a masterpiece overnight. In fact, he had approximately 10 years of rejected paintings before he painted his first masterpiece "Les Demoiselles d'Avignon" in 1907.

The greatest lesson that can be learned from Picasso is that a masterpiece is possible with persistence. Imagine if he would have given up, believing he would be no more than a broke painter who had to burn his drawings for warmth. We would never have had the opportunity to experience his great works entitled, Nude, Green Leaves and Bust, Asleep, Le Reve (The Dream), Blue Nude and so many more. He experienced many successes after great failures.

That too can be the case for our young people. A masterpiece lies within! Without our persistence we may never discover that masterpiece. We may never see the possibility of these young people becoming doctors, lawyers, orators, artists, businessmen, and yes, even the President of the United States of America. Their possibilities are endless. However, many of our young people don't recognize all the buried treasures that lie within them because either they've never been told of them or perhaps they've forgotten because of the voices that say they can't. Our job is to hand them a paint brush and assist them in painting a picture that will go against U.S. statistics, community norms, and popular opinions. Unfortunately, they have painted the pictures they have seen, and replicating the pictures of their environment, but it is our job to teach them how to paint pictures that include a quality education, a healthy lifestyle, and a bright future.

Painting allows do overs. In the world of painting, nothing is permanent, anything can be undone. One of the greatest things about painting is that you can paint over something that's not working.

Many TV shows have become

> Painting allows do overs.

popular for taking household pieces like old junk, furniture and stuff that has been in one's basement or garage for years and then recreating it into something stunning and of worth.

You can paint over an old cabinet and make it look new again.

You can paint over a drab color that doesn't bring the picture to life and create something with pizazz.

You can take what has seemed to be garbage to some and create a masterpiece.

In fact, in one of Pablo Picasso's first masterpieces, "The Blue Room," scientists have discovered another painting just underneath the surface: a portrait of an old man resting his head in his hands. It has been said that due to Picasso's earlier portraits not resulting in sells, he would paint over his works until one would sell.

I can't help but think of the image that was found underneath "The Blue Room." For me, this image of an old man resting his head in his hands suggests one who is tired, perhaps void of dreams, hope, and aspirations. Then, Picasso paints over this and creates a refreshing and rejuvenating portrait that is known for its natural light capturing a young woman bathing in a tub, which would suggest to me that she is becoming refreshed and renewed in preparation for a day of productivity and goal chasing. A masterpiece is created from an obscure beginning.

Just as Picasso's first picture didn't suggest potential, the current image of our youth doesn't necessarily resemble a picture that has great potential. We see the statistics that seem impossible to reverse, environments not conducive for positive growth, family dysfunctions and tragic cycles and so we believe that these young people in such situations are unlikely to become anything different than their environments and predicaments. In fact, the term "at risk youth" suggests that these particular groups of adolescents are less likely to transition successfully into adulthood and achieve economic self-sufficiency. According to the American Leadership Forum, one in three African-American and one in six Hispanic boys born in 2001 are at risk of becoming part of the prison population.

These are facts that have good evidence to support them. However, I believe that with the proper intervention, even "at risk", African-American and Hispanic youth can become masterpieces. The picture can be reworked and redone, just like Picasso's masterpiece.

Picasso said, *"What comes out in the end is the result of discarded finds."* What does this mean? As I considered these words, I came to the conclusion that Picasso was saying that the best masterpieces are those that are reworked and created from what has been rejected or considered unusable.

So, guess what? Our inner-city urban youth have the possibility of becoming the best masterpieces. Maybe some will require a lot of reworking and some will require less, but none are a lost cause. We must take the picture that has already been painted and let it serve as a new inspiration. You may have noticed I said, WE! Yes, me and you. It's our responsibility, since we are only one, "to do the something that we can do" and that something is to reframe the world of inner-city youth, without judgment or criticism.

One of my duties while working with the detention alternative program was to create ISP's (Individualized Service Plans) for youth in the juvenile justice program. This document would create a plan for advocates on how to best provide intervention for the adolescent. However, in order to complete this task I had to review their rap sheets, files that were often thicker than a novel. These files would contain information that would suggest that this youth is a lost cause. They're often full of court dockets, unsuccessful treatment plans, violations of probation, burglary charges, gun charges, joy riding charges, drug charges, high school dropout documents, runaway notes, and numerous write-ups describing an adolescent who is least likely to succeed. Quite often, the juvenile court system is simply waiting for the adolescent to age out as they are predetermined to serve real time in prison, so great intervention isn't completed for this group.

However, in my experience, I've learned and practiced not to read the files before meeting the youth. Of course, I'm not always able to prevent myself from hearing the opinions of my colleagues regarding the youth, but I've learned how to ignore it and develop my own assessment. So, I would spend two to four weeks getting to know the adolescent and not the file. In the two to four weeks I would learn that they have hearts, aspirations, and hopes. I would learn that they are looking for love, desire attention, and long for mentorship. I learned that they are worth fighting

EVERY young person is of worth.

for, so I would fight for them. I've lost some battles, but I've certainly won more. Even after being hurt, burnt, and taken advantage of, I am still convinced that EVERY young person is of worth. Seeing as though they're currently hanging out on corners, sagging their pants, speaking inappropriate slang, cussing like sailors, disrespectful, and lacking focus, I'll admit that their pictures can be unpleasant. Nonetheless, it doesn't mean they're not of worth and neither does it mean they can't become works of art. In actuality, they're already a masterpiece that desperately needs dusting off, resurfacing, and reworking.

A Microsoft commercial announced, "It may not be obvious yet but one of these kids are going to change the world. We just got to make sure they have what they need." It may not be obvious, in fact many times it can be difficult to see. The statistics can be more obvious than the potential of a masterpiece in the making. However, the unobvious is always the best gift. I'm one who enjoys surprises and there's a certain emotion that is invoked when the unobvious becomes manifested. I've had the opportunity to work with youth where the possibility of them improving their lives was not obvious, but when it happens, and it does; it produces an inexpressible feeling and joy like none other. So I say, it is possible to paint a better picture, to change a life, to create a new destiny. I often tell the young people I meet, "The picture that has been painted for you is not the picture you have to paint for yourself."

Artist Bob Ross said, "All you need to paint is a few tools, a little instruction, and a vision in your mind."

We have to provide the tools, convey the instructions, and help cultivate the vision. We must teach them how to paint it, frame it, and hang it.

> We must teach them how to paint it, frame it, and hang it.

Beginning the project of painting is sometimes the hardest step because many don't believe they have what is required. It is our job to remind them that they too were born with the tools to become great but of no fault of their own, those tools weren't kept safe, sharpened, and nurtured. Thus, the tools simply need to be uncovered as they are buried but not gone.

Another method that painters use to rework a painting is to first scrape off the old paint. So that's what we do in the life of the youth, we come in and start scraping off the old paint. We scrape and scrape and scrape. We scrape off the moments that created the feelings of despair and not feeling of worth. We scrape off the residue from fatherless homes. We scrape off the belief that life hasn't been fair to them. We scrape off the thoughts that suggest prison is part of their future. We scrape off the grave images of them being killed and not living long lives. And while we're scrapping, we too are convincing the young person that we are pursuing their best interests, and that we're in it for the long haul. Unfortunately, they've had so many people and programs come in and out of their lives that it has now caused them to shut down and become resistant to help. That doesn't mean we retreat, it simply means we work harder. I told you it wouldn't be easy, but it is so worth it.

So after much scraping is done, you may still not have scraped it all off. Be sure to scrape the darkest areas, otherwise they will be sure to resurface through the new paint. Now, it's time to re-paint, refinish, and restore! Restore the dreams of childhood that were stolen by the streets. Restore the dream of having a family that was stolen by dysfunctional homes. Restore the dream of having a successful career that was destroyed by their poverty stricken environments. Paint a new picture. A picture that tells a story of becoming a high school graduate, becoming a college graduate, becoming a successful professional, becoming a masterpiece.

After painting, we must then help them frame the vision. A frame is meant to protect a picture. After all the hard work, you do not want the picture destroyed, bent, or torn, so you frame it. Framing it suggests that it's worth keeping because no one frames junk. We reserve frames for things that are valuable. The future of our youth is valuable so we remind them of that and ensure that there is a circle of support (a frame) to ensure their continued success. It's pointless to make a huge investment and then walk away. A wise investor follows his investment and makes every effort to ensure its growth. We must do the same for our youth. It is so easy for them to return to what they know. This is why we protect it with a frame that provides supreme support. I am not in favor of programs that will work with a young person for three months or six months and leave them without another referral or support system. That's like painting a picture and not framing it. Our youth need on-going support. Many mentoring programs suggest that dramatic progress and results are not shown until after two years. Continued support is essential.

Just as I'm writing, I received a text from one of my mentees that I have been working with for over seven years. The text reads:

"Thank you for always being there for me and always being a genuinely great person. You are a huge influence whether you see it or not. I will make you proud!"

I work hard to ensure that even after seven years, this young person still understands that I am here for him. While the level of support may decrease, support is continually needed.

Lastly, we hang the picture. Framing it is one thing, but hanging it means another. Hanging the picture sets it above the rest. It provides a constant reminder of what the picture conveys and a reminder of what they will become. It represents the writing of their story. They need to constantly know that this picture will become their reality, so we hang it as a reminder of their promising future. We hang it by reminding them how proud we are of them, and how much we expect from them. I replied to the young man's text and said, "I'm already proud of you and look forward to seeing all that you become!" I reminded him of how far he's come and how he's on a journey to greatness. I constantly hang the picture. There's a phrase, "to hang over one's head." That phrase is usually perceived as a negative, but here I see it to be positive. We hang the new picture that has been created over the heads of our youth, so that they always have insight about where they are headed and what they have to do to get there. We acknowledge it often. Even more, we celebrate their future before others. We tell the world and it becomes special news. Ironically, our news channels and newspapers are quick to broadcast the negative activities that occur with our youth. Rarely do we see the brighter pictures being hung. We can't wait on the media to recognize them, for it is our job to do so. My young people love when I take a picture of them and post it on my social media pages with a caption conveying their progress. For them, it's me hanging the new picture that has been painted for all to see. It reminds them that in spite of what others say or what they have done, they are still good and of significant worth.

Christian doctrine states: God painted a magnificent picture from the void. In other words, a world that had little potential, before you knew it, stars appeared. Our earth and its moon hung in the sky, waters flowed, grass sprouted, animals were made, and living creatures were produced. Who would have thought something so amazing could come from something so dark, so formless, and so void. A better picture was painted! Now I'm not saying that we are God, but I am saying we too can take the 'least likely,' 'disadvantaged,' 'lost causes,' and paint a better picture for them and watch a masterpiece be created from rejected beginnings. Then, the world can no longer call our kids bad or lost causes, but they must say like God did in the Christian story of creation: "It is good!"

Painting Pictures Challenge: When I go to speak at schools and youth functions, I take a canvas for youth to paint their picture. For some that means writing their goals and others actually draw what they desire to become. I've seen many amazing dreams that are achievable conveyed on these canvases. I have provided a page with a frame that is waiting for a picture. Draw, write or color your vision for the youth you work with or will work with. Then, implement it.

Painting Pictures
REFRAMING THE WORLD OF INNER-CITY YOUTH

EPILOGUE: LOOK INTO THEIR EYES

"The eyes shout what the lips fear to say."

- William Henry

We know the stories, we know the statistics, and we know the need for support. As expressed in earlier chapters, simply knowing isn't enough. The response to knowing makes the biggest difference in the life of a young person. If after reading this book, you still aren't convinced that inner-city youth have talent, potential, and positive dreams, then I challenge you.

My last and final challenge.

I challenge you to look into their eyes. Their appearance may tell the story of the street life: sagging jeans, tough tattoos and a bad attitude, but their eyes do not lie, and they all hunger for something more. Their defiant behavior may seem justified in the difficult world of poverty and violence where it is a struggle not to become a victim of the streets, but provide an opportunity, resources, and support, and their behavior will change for the better. As they mimic the images around them, their behavior and appearance disguise what they feel and dream.

If you look into their eyes, you'll see that they are afraid. Although they'll suggest that they don't mind dying or going to jail, their eyes are in disagreement. Their eyes say they're afraid to go home to a broken house, they're afraid to hear more tragic news of a friend or a family member lost. They're afraid to be seen at night as they too might fall victim.

If you look into their eyes, you'll learn that they really want out of the 'street life,' but then the feeling of hopelessness only incites anger and frustration. Their anger and emotion escapes in many ways, most of the time in rebellious anti-authoritative ways, which in turn gets them into trouble. We see the anger and frustration in those they mock and bully – perhaps a student doing well in a class that the youth is failing. Or they intimidate a person with expensive clothes because they believe they'll never attain the luxury. They truly wish that they could obtain a professional career that would provide them with respect and dignity.

If you look into their eyes, you'll learn that they really want your help. In spite of their resistance, the non-compliance, and the inconsistencies, they really do want someone to care about them, help them, and love them. Many of our kids don't feel loved or have heard anyone say, "I LOVE YOU." If you look really closely, their eyes are saying, "don't give up on me - stick it out – bear with me," because this will ultimately prove to them that they are worth it.

Look into their eyes, but not with a superficial lens, judging them for one thing or another. Look deeper with your heart, as if they are your child, brother, sister, nephew, niece, or cousin. Look into their eyes as though you know that they are your future.

WORKS CITED

Alexander, Reginald. "Inner City Mayhem: The Lures, Causes, and Effects of Inner-City Drug-Dealing." *Drug War Prisoners*. 1998. 10 November 2015.

Carlie, Mike. *Into The Abyss: A Personal Journey into the World of Street Gangs*. Springfield, MO: M. Carlie, 2002.

Castillo, Mariano. "Is a New Crime Wave on the Horizon." *CNN*. Cable News Network, 4 June 2015. Web. 05 November 2015.

Hurt, Hallam, Elsa Malmud, Nancy L. Brodsky, and Joan Giannetta. "Arch Pediatr Adolesc Med -- Abstract: Exposure to Violence: Psychological and Academic Correlates in Child Witnesses, December 2001, Hurt Et Al. 155 (12): 1351." *Archives of Pediatrics & Adolescent Medicine, a Monthly Peer-reviewed Medical Journal Published by AMA*. N.p., 2001. Web. 8 October 2015.

Holman, Barry, and Jason Ziedenberg. *The Dangers of Detention: The Impact of Incarcerating Youth in Detention and Other Secure Facilities*. Washington, D.C.: Justice Policy Institute, 2006. Print.

Johnson, Mason. "Chicago's Failure to Lower Homicides, Here's What We Need To Do." *CBS Chicago*. N.p., 2 Oct. 2015. Web. 8 October 2015.

Liderson, Kary, and Carlos J. Ortiz. "More Young People Are Killed in Chicago than Any Other American City." *Chicago Reporter*. N.p., 25 Jan. 2012. Web. 5 October 2015.

Mosely, E. "*GO KIDS* Articles." GO KIDS. N.p., 6 July 2008. Web. 1 October 2015.

Ratliff, Adam. "Most Justice-Involved Youth Affected by Traumatic Childhood Experiences." *Justice Policy Institute.* Justice Policy Institute, 7 July 2010. Web. 8 October 2015.

Rhodes, Steve. "Prison Vs. College." *NBC Chicago.* NBC, n.d. Web. 8 October 2015.

Schaefer, Paula. "Girls in the Juvenile Justice System." *Girls in the Juvenile Justice System.* N.p., 2008. Web. 15 December 2015.

Shumba, Rabison. "The Importance of Exposure in Life." *Ezinearticles.com.* N.p., 23 July 2010. Web. 3 October 2015.

Stiglitz, Joseph. "Equal Opportunity, Our National Myth." *The New York Times.* N.p., 16 Feb. 2013. Web. 1 October 2015.

Thomas, Jerry, and Steve Johnson. "Getting Out Of Gang Tougher Than Saying, `I Quit`." *Tribunedigita.* Chicago Tribune. N.p., 12 Sept. 1991. Web. 3 September 2015.

"Data." *American Community Survey.* United States Census Bureau, n.d. Web. 3 September 2015.

"Girls Health and Justice Institute." *Girls Health and Justice Institute.* N.p., n.d. Web. 1 December 2015.

"High School Graduation Rates Rise in Some Major U.S. Cities, But Significant Work Remains to Curb Dropout Crisis." *America's Promise.* America's Promise Alliance, 22 Apr. 2009. Web. 1 September 2015.

"Healing Invisible Wounds: Why Investing in Trauma-Informed Care for Children Makes Sense." *Justice Policy Institute.* Justice Policy Institute, July 2010. Web. 3 September 2015.

"*Juvenile Offenders and Victims: 2014 National Report* (Report Summary)."Juvenile Offenders and Victims: 2014 National Report. U.S. Department of Justice, 2014. Web. 22 July 2015.

"*National Youth Gang Survey Analysis.*" National Youth Gang Survey Analysis. National Gang Center, n.d. Web. 15 Nov. 2015.

"*National Criminal Justice Reference Service*, NCJRS." National Criminal Justice Reference Service. N.p., n.d. Web. 3 September 2015.

"The Impact of School Suspensions, and a Demand for Passage of the Student Safety Act | *New York Civil Liberties Union (NYCLU) - American Civil Liberties Union of New York State.*" New York Civil Liberties Union (NYCLU) - American Civil Liberties Union of New York State. New York Civil Liberties Union, n.d. Web. 3 September 2015.

"*WebMD Infertility Center*: Trying to Conceive, Symptoms, Causes in Men and Women, Tests, and Treatments." WebMD. WebMD, n.d. Web. 8 June 2015.

NOTES

NOTES

NOTES

NOTES

NOTES

NOTES

NOTES

ABOUT THE BOOK

Growing up in disadvantaged neighborhoods, our youth learn at an early age that they have to adapt to the rules of the streets or fall victim to it. Thus, they replicate the image of their environment, resulting in the ongoing cycle of violence, drugs, incarceration and tragedy. This book brings you into the harsh and complex world in which our urban youth struggle and you will hear first-hand accounts of the alarming images and circumstances inner-city youth must overcome. You will learn that although their pictures look bleak, filled with disasters, frustrations and destructive emotions, a greater picture can be painted. Tear-jerking testimonies will provide an understanding that even those raised in the most hopeless of environments can still grow and evolve into sources of inspiration for their community and for society. Painting Pictures serves to remind us all that we can play a crucial role in ensuring that our marginalized youth receive the support and encouragement they need to rise out of their poor conditions and paint a better future for themselves.